5
4.95

THE MARK OF THE BEAST

By

SYDNEY WATSON

Author of "In the Twinkling of An Eye";
"Scarlet and Purple"

FLEMING H. REVELL COMPANY

PUBLISHER'S NOTE.

AFTER the Lord's Second Coming, what will happen to those left behind? What will the Tribulation period be like? What will happen during the reign of the Antichrist? What is meant by "The Mark of the Beast"? What will be the fate of those who refuse to bear this mark?

All of these questions and many others connected with the mark of the beast, are answered in this realistic, startling, awe-inspiring story.

Although entirely fictional, the author has based his narrative on just what the Bible teaches concerning the Great Tribulation—that awful period of distress and woe that is coming upon this earth during the time when the Antichrist will rule with unhindered sway. It is a story you will never forget—a story that has been used of God in the salvation of souls, and in awakening careless Christians to the need of a closer walk with Jesus in their daily lives. This volume deserves a wide reading. It should be in every Sunday School Library and in every home.

To that Champion of "The Word of God,

THE

Rev. G. CAMPBELL MORGAN, D.D.

THIS BOOK IS

(BY HIS PERMISSION) HUMBLY

Dedicated,

IN RECOGNITION OF THE SPIRITUAL HELP,

AND A DEEP QUICKENING

TO BIBLE STUDY RECEIVED BY THE

AUTHOR

CONTENTS.

PREFACE.

PROLOGUE.

PREFACE.

THE great acceptance with which the Author's previous volume "In the Twinkling of an Eye" was received, when published in Oct. 1910, together with the many records of blessing resulting from the perusal, leads him to hope that the present volume may prove equally useful.

The subjects treated in this volume are possibly less known, (even among *some* who hold the truth of the Lord's *Near* Return in joyful Hope) than the subjects handled "In the Twinkling of an Eye," but they certainly should have as much interest as the earlier truths, and should lead (those hitherto unacquainted with them) to a careful, prayerful searching of "The Word."

The Author would here mark his indebtedness to Dr. Joseph A. Seiss, and Dr. Campbell Morgan, for the inceptive thoughts *re* Judas Iscariot, and The Antichrist. Dr. Campbell Morgan's very remarkable sermon on "Christ and Judas"—under date December 18, 1908—while being profoundly interesting and illuminating, it has proved to the Author to be the only sound theory of explanation of that perplexing personality—Judas Iscariot—he has ever met.

While cleaving close to Scripture, at the same time it has settled the life-long perplexity of the writer of this book, as to the difficulties surrounding "The Traitor."

The fictional form has again been adopted in this volume, for the same reasons that obtained in the writing of "In the Twinkling of an Eye." The use of the fictional style for the presentment of sacred subjects is ever a moot-point with some people. Yet, every parable, allegory, etc., (not excepting Bunyan's Master-piece) is *fictional* form. So that the moot-point really becomes one *of degree* and not of *principle—if* Bunyan, Milton, and Dante, be allowed to be right. Certain it is that many thousands have read, and have been awakened, quickened, even converted, by reading "In the Twinkling of an Eye," "Long Odds," "He's coming To-morrow," (Mrs. Harriet Beecher Stowe) who would never have looked at an ordinary pamphlet or book upon the subject. One of the truest and most noted leaders (in the "Church") on our great convention platforms, himself an authority, and voluminous writer on the *pre*-milleniarian view of our Lord's near Return, (a perfect stranger, personally, to the writer) wrote within a week or two of the issue of "In the Twinkling of an Eye," saying:

"I have just finished reading your *wonderful* book "In the Twinkling of an Eye." It has *solemnised* me *very greatly*—more than anything for a long time . . . . May the Lord use your book to *STARTLE* the careless, ill-taught professing Christians . . . Please send me 24 copies, etc., etc."

The desire of the author of "The Mark of the Beast" has been to further "startle" and awaken "careless, il' taught *professing* Christians," by giving some faint view of the fate of those *professors* who will be *"left behind"* to go through the horrors of The Tribulation.

To be true to his subject, and to his convictions, the author has had to approach one or two *delicate* subjects. These he has sought to touch in a veiled, a guarded way. Each reader, if desirous of pursuing more minutely the study of those special parts, can do so by referring to other Christian author's works.

That there is a growing interest in the whole subject of "The Lord's Coming," is very apparent in many ways. The intense interest and quickening that has accompanied the Author's many series of Bible Readings on "The Near Return of our Lord," during the past twelve months especially, would have proved the revived interest in the subject—if proof had been needed.

SYDNEY WATSON.

"The Firs," Vernham Dean. Hungerford, Berks. April 24th, 1911.

THE MARK OF THE BEAST

PROLOGUE.

IT was late August. The year 18—— no matter the exact date, except that the century was growing old. A small house-party was gathered under the sixteenth century roof of that fine old Warwickshire house, "The Antlers."

"Very old famerly, very old!" the head coachman was fond of saying to sight-seers, and others. "Come over with William of Normandy, the first Duerdon did. Famerly allus kept 'emselves very eleck, cream-del-al-cream, as the saying is in hupper cirkles."

The coachman's estimate of the Duerdon House will serve all the purpose we need here, and enable us to move among the guests of the house-party though we have little to do save with two of them—the most striking female personality in the house, Judith Montmarte, and the latest society lion, Colonel Youlter, the Thibet explorer.

Judith Montmarte, as her name suggests, was a Jewess. She was tall—it is curious that the nineteen centuries of Semitic persecution should have left the Jewess taller, in proportion, than the Jew—Judith Montmarte was tall, with a full figure. The contour of her face suggested Spanish blood. Her hair—what a wealth of it there was—was blue-black, finer than such hair usually is, and with a sheen on it like unto a raven's wing. Her eyes were large, black, and melting in their fullness. Her lips were full, and rich in their crimson.

The face was extraordinarily beautiful, in a general way. But though the lips and eyes would be accounted lovely, yet a true student of faces would have read cruelty in the ruby lips, and a shade of hell lurking in the melting black eyes. A millionairess, several times over, (if report could be trusted) she was known and felt to be a powerful personage. There was not a continental or oriental court where she was not well-known —and feared, because of her power. A much·travelled woman, a wide reader—especially in the matter of the occult; a superb musician; a Patti and a Lind rolled into one, made her the most wonderful songster of the day.

In character—chameleon is the only word that can in anyway describe her. As regarded her appearances in society, her acceptance of invitations, etc., she was usually regarded as capricious, to a fault. But this was as it *appeared* to those with whom she had to do. She had been known to refuse a banquet at the table of a prince, yet eat a dish of macaroni with a peasant, or boiled chestnuts with a forest charcoal burner. What the world did not know, did not realize, was that, in these things, she was not capricious, but simply serving some deep purpose of her life.

She had accepted the Duerdon invitation because she specially desired to meet Colonel Youlter.

To-night, the pair had met for the first time, just five minutes before the gong had sounded for dinner. Colonel Youlter had taken her down to the dining-room.

Just at first she had spoken but little, and the Colonel had thought her fatigued, for he had caught one glimpse of the dreamy languor in her great liquid eyes.

An almost chance remark of his, towards the end of the meal, anent the mysticism, the spiritism of the East, and the growing cult of the same order in the West, appeared to suddenly wake her from her dreaminess. Her dark eyes were turned quickly up to his, a new and eager light flashed in them.

"Do you know," she said, her tone low enough to be caught only by him, "that it was only the expectation of meeting you, and hearing you talk of the occult, of that wondrous mysticism of the East, that made me accept the invitation to this house——that is, I should add, at this particular time, for I *had* arranged to go to my glorious Hungarian hills this week."

Colonel Youlter searched her face eagerly. Had she spoken the tongue of flattery, or of the mere conventional? He saw she had not, and he began to regard her with something more than the mere curiosity with which he had anticipated meeting her.

In his callow days he had been romantic to a degree. Even now his heart was younger than his years, for while he had never wed, because of a love-tragedy thirty years before, he had preserved a rare, a very tender chivalry towards women. He knew he would never love again, as he had once loved, though, at times, he told himself that he might yet love in a soberer fashion, and even wed.

"You are interested in the occult, Miss Montmarte?" he replied.

She smiled up into his face, as she said:

" 'Interested,' Colonel Youlter? interested is no word for it, for I might almost say that it is a passion with me, for very little else in life really holds me long, compared with my love for it."

She glanced swiftly to right and left, and across the table to see if she was being watched, or listened to. Everyone seemed absorbed with either their plates or their companions.

Bending towards the man at her side, she said, "You know what an evening is like at such times as this. We women will adjourn to the Drawing Room, you men will presently join us, there will be a buzzing of voices, talk— 'cackle' one of America's representatives used to term it, and it was a good name, only that the hen has done something to cackle about, she has fulfilled the purpose for which she came into existence, and women—the average Society women, at least—do not. Then there'll be singing, of a sort, and—but you know, Colonel, all the usual rigmarole. Now I want a long, long talk with you about the subject you have just broached. We could not talk, as we would, in the crowd that will be in the drawing-room presently, so I wonder if you would give me an hour in the library, tomorrow morning after breakfast. I suggest the library because I find it is the one room in the house into which no one ever seems to go. Of course, Colonel Youlter, if you have something else you must needs do in the forenoon, pray don't regard my suggestion. Or, if you would prefer that we walked and talked, I will gladly accommodate myself to your time and your conveniences."

He assured her that he had made no plans for the morrow, and that he would be delighted to meet her in the library, for a good long 'confab' over the subject that evidently possessed a mutual attraction for them.

Mentally, while he studied her, he decided that her chief charm, in his eyes, was her absolute naturalness and unconventionality. "But to some men," he mused "what a danger zone she would prove. Allied to her great beauty, her wealth, and her gifts, there is a way with her that would make her almost absolutely irresistible if she had set her heart on anything!"

An hour later that opinion deepened within him as he listened to her singing in the drawing-room. She had been known to bluntly, flatly refuse an Emperor who had asked her to sing, and yet to take a little Sicillian street singer's tambourine from her hand, and sing the coppers and silver out of the pockets of the folk who had crowded the market-place at the first liquid notes of her song. She rarely sang in the houses of her hosts and hostesses. Tonight she had voluntarily gone to the piano, accompanying herself.

She sang in Hungarian, a folk-song, and a love song of the people of her own land. Yearning and wistful, full of that curious mystical melancholy, that always appealed to her own soul, and which characterizes some of the oldest of the Hungarian folk-songs.

Her second song finished, amid the profoundest hush, she rose as suddenly from the piano as she had seated herself. A little later she was missed from the company. She had slipped away to her room, after a quiet good-night to her table-companion, Colonel Youlter.

*   *   *   *   *

At ten-thirty, next morning, Judith Montmarte entered the library. The Colonel was there already. He rose to meet her, saying, "Where will you sit? Where will you be most comfortable."

There was a decidedly "comfo" air about the luxuriously-furnished room. The eyes of the beautiful woman —she was twenty-eight—swept the apartment and, finally, resting upon a delightful *vis-a-vis*, she laughed merrily, as she said:

"Fancy finding a *vis-a-vis*, and of this luxurious type, too, in a library. I always think it is a mistake to have the library of the house so stiff, sometimes the library is positively forbidding."

She laughed lightly again, as she said. "I'm going off into a disquisition on interiors, so—shall we sit here?"

She dropped into one of the curves of the *vis-a-vis*, and he took the other.

For half-an-hour their talk on their pet subject was more or less general, then he startled her by asking:

"Do you know the Christian New Testament, at all?"

"The Gospels, I have read," she replied, "and am fairly well familiar with them. I have read, too, the final book, "The Revelation," which though a sealed book to me, as far as knowledge of its meaning goes, yet has, I confess, a perennial attraction for me."

She lifted her great eyes to his, a little quizzical expression in them, as she added:

"You are surprised that I, a Jewess, should speak thus of the Gentile scriptures!"

Then, without giving him time to reply, she went on:

"But why did you ask whether I knew anything of the New Testament?"

"Because, apropos of what I said a moment ago, anent the repetition of History, the Christ of the New Testament declared that "as the days of Noah were, so shall also the coming of the Son of Man be.""

She nodded her beautiful head, as though she would assent to the correctness of his quotation.

"Now I make no profession of being ultra-Christian," he went on, "but I know the *letter* of the Bible quite as well as most Teachers of Christianity, and without intending any egotism I am sure I dare to say that I know it infinitely better than the average Christian. And if I *was* a teacher or preacher of the Christian faith I would raise my voice most vehemently against the wilful, sinful ignorance of the Bible on the part of the professed Christians. Members of the various so-called 'churches,' seem to know *every*thing *except* their Bibles. Mention a passage in Spenser, William Wordsworth, Whittier, Longfellow, Tennyson, Browning, or even Swinburne, William Watson, Charles Fox, Carleton, or Lowell, and they can pick the volume off the shelf in an instant, and the next instant, they have the book open at your quotation. But quote Jude or Enoch, or Job on salt with our eggs, and they go fumbling about in the mazes of Leviticus, or the Minor Prophets."

He laughed, not maliciously, but with a certain pitying contempt, as he said:

"The average *professing* Christian is about as much like the New Testament model of what he should be, as

is the straw-stuffed scarecrow in the field, in the pockets
of the costume of which the birds conceive it to be the
latest joke to build. But I am digressing, I was beginning
about the 'days of Noah' and their *near* future repetition
on the earth."

" *'Near repetition?'* How do you mean, Colonel?"
Judith Montmarte leaned a little eagerly toward him. In
the ordinary way, alone with a man of his type she
would have played the coquette. To-day she thought
nothing of such trifling. There was something so different in his manner, as he spoke of the things that were
engaging them, to even the ordinary preacher.

The pair were as utterly alone as though they had been
on the wide, wide sea together in an open boat. She had
said truly, over-night, "no one ever comes near the
library."

"I mean," he said, replying to her question, "that the
seven chief causes of the apostasy which brought down
God's wrath upon the Antediluvians, have already begun
to manifest themselves upon the earth, in such a measure
as to warrant one's saying that 'as it was in the days of
Noah, so it is again today,' and if the New Testament
is true in every letter—we may expect the Return of the
Christ at any moment."

She was staring amazedly at him—enquiring, eager,
but evidently puzzled. But she made no sound or sign
of interruption, and he went on:

"The first element of the Antediluvian apostasy was
the worship of God as Creator and Benefactor, and not
as the Jehovah-God of Covenant and Mercy. And surely
that is what we find everywhere to-day. People acknowledge a Supreme Being, and accept Christ as a model man,
but they flatly deny the Fall, Hereditary Sin, the need

of an Atonement, and all else that is connected with the Great Evangel. The *Second* cause of Antediluvian apostasy was the disregard of the original law of marriage, and the increased prominence of the female sex."

Judith Montmarte smiled back into his face, as she said:

"Oh that you would propound that in a convention of New Women! And yet—yet—yes, you are right, as to your fact, as regards life, to-day."

The pair had a merry, friendly spar for a moment or two, then, at her request, he resumed his subject, and, for a full half hour, he amazed her with his comparisons of the Antediluvian age with the present time. He was an interesting speaker and she enjoyed the time immensely. But, presently, when he came to his seventh and last likeness between the two ages, since it had to do with a curious phase of Spiritism, she became more intensely interested.

"There seems to me," he said, "but one correct way of interpreting that historical item of those strange, Antediluvian days: 'The sons of God saw the daughters of men that they were fair; and they took them wives of all which they chose.' The superficial rendering of this, sometimes given, that it signifies nothing more than the intermarriage of Cainites and Sethites, will not suffice when a deeper examination is made in the original languages. The term 'Sons of God' does not appear to have any other meaning in the *Old* Testament, than that of angels.

"Some of the angels, with Lucifer, fell from their high estate in Heaven, and were banished from Heaven. Scripture clearly proves in many places that these fallen ones took up their abode 'in the air,' the Devil becoming even as the Christ Himself said: 'Prince of the power of the air.'

"Now both Peter and Jude, in their epistles allude to certain of these fallen, air-dwelling angels, leaving their first estate, and the mention of their *second* fall is sufficiently clear to indicate their sin—intermarriage with the fairest of the daughters of men. Their name as given in the old Testament, 'Nephilim' means 'fallen ones.' In their original condition, as angels in Heaven, they 'neither married nor were given in marriage.' It is too big a subject, Miss Judith ——."

Hurriedly, eagerly, for she wanted him to continue his topic, she said:

"Call me Ju, or Judith, or Judy, Colonel, and drop the 'Miss,' and do please go on with this very wonderful subject."

"Thank you, Ju," he laughed, then continuing his talk, he said:

"It is far too big a subject, Ju, in all its details, to talk of here and now, but, broadly, the fact seems to me to remain, that fallen angels assumed human shape, or in some way held illicit intercourse with the women of the day, a race of giant-like beings resulting. For this foul sin God would seem to have condemned these doubly sinning fallen angels to Tartarus, to be reserved unto Judgment.

" 'Now as it was in the days of Noah, so shall it be in the coming of the Son of Man,' and——"

Judith Montmarte caught her breath sharply, and, in an unconscious movement of eager wonder, let her beautiful hand drop upon his wrist, as she gasped "you don't think—you don't mean—er—er—, tell me, Colonel, do you mean to say that—"

"I do mean," he replied, "that I am firmly convinced that so far has demonology increased—the door being opened by modern spiritualism—that I believe this poor old world of ours is beginning to experience a return of this association between fallen spirits and the daughters of men. Of course, I cannot enter into minute detail with *you*, Ju, but let me register my firm conviction, that I believe from some such demoniacal association, there will spring the 'Man of Sin'—'The Antichrist.'

At that instant, to the utter amaze of both of them, the first luncheon gong sounded. They had been talking for nearly three hours. With the request from Judith, and a promise from him to resume the subject at the first favourable opportunity, they parted.

Intensely, almost feverishly excited, Judith went to her room. Beautiful in face and form as she was, she was fouler than a Lucretia Borgia, in soul, in thought. And now, as a foul, wild, mad thought surged through her brain, she murmured, half-aloud:

"Demon or man, what matters! If I thought I could be the Mother of The Antichrist, I would—so much do I hate the Nazarene, the Christ—."

She spat through the open window as she uttered the precious, though to her the hated name of the Son of God.

CHAPTER 1.

TWENTY-FIVE YEARS LATER.

THE huge London church was crowded in every part, and men had been standing in the aisles from the first moment that the service began. The preacher who had attracted so huge a crowd at two-thirty on a weekday afternoon, was one of the very youngest of the "coming men" of the English church. Tall, thin, with a magnificent head crowned by a mane of hair that was fast becoming prematurely grey, and a face so intense in its cast, and set with eyes so piercing, that strangers, not knowing who he was, would almost inevitably turn to look at him when they passed him on the street. His career had been a strange one. Ordained at quite an early age, he had been offered a living within six months of his ordination. He entered upon his charge, preached but once only, then met with an accident that laid him low for seven years. The seven years were fruitful years, since, shut up with God and His word, he had become almost the most remarkable spiritually-minded Bible student of his time.

The day came, at length, when once more he was strong enough to do public service, and though without a living, from the moment that he had preached his first sermon, after his recovery, he found himself in constant request on every hand. He lived in close communion with God, and his soul burned within him as he delivered —not an address, not a sermon, but the *message of God*.

The music of the voluntary was filling all the church, while the offering was being taken. Then, as the last well-filled plate was piled on the step of the communion rail, the voluntary died away in a soft whisper. Amid a tense hush, he rose to give out the hymn before the sermon. Clear, bell-like, his voice rang out:

"When I survey the wondrous cross."

The hymn sung, he gave out his text: "Did not I choose you the twelve, and one of you *is* a demon."

"You will note," he began "that I have changed the word devil to demon. There is but one devil in the universe, but there are myriads of demons, fallen angels like their master, the Devil, only they were angels of lesser rank."

He paused for one moment, and his eagle eyes swept the sea of faces. Then in quiet, calm, but incisive tones he asked:

"Who,—what, was Judas Iscariot? Was he *human*, was he man, as I am, as you are? or, was he a demon? Jesus Christ our Lord, who knew as God, as well as man, declared that Judas was a *demon*—a fallen angel.

The silence was awesome in its tenseness. Every eye was fixed on the preacher, necks were strained forward, lips were parted—the people held their breath.

Again that clear, rich bell-like voice rang out in the repeated question: "Who, I repeat, was Judas Iscariot? Was he a man, in the usual acceptance of the term, or was he a demon incarnated? What does the Bible say about him? In considering this I ask you each to put from your mind, as far as it is possible for you to do so, all preconceived ideas, all that you have been accustomed to think about this flame of evil in the story of Christ.

"And first let me say what my own feeling, my own strong personal conviction is regarding Judas Iscariot. I believe him to have been a demon incarnated by the power of the Devil, whose intent was to frustrate God's plans. In all his foul work of destruction and confusion, the Devil, from the time of the Fall in Eden, has ever been busy counterfeiting all that God has wrought out for the salvation of the human race, and as the time approaches for his own utter defeat so the more cunning will his devices of evil become.

"In the foulness of his thoughts to frustrate God's purposes of salvation, I believe that when he knew that the Christ had been born, that God had Himself become incarnate, so that He might deliver man—for we must never forget that 'God was in Christ reconciling the world unto Himself'—that he, the Devil, incarnated one of his demons, who afterwards became known as Judas Iscariot, the Betrayer of Christ."

For one instant the preacher paused, for the awed and listening mass of people who had been literally holding their breath, were compelled to inbreathe, and the catch of breath was heard through all the place.

"To use a twentieth century expression," he went on, "I may seem to have 'given myself away' by this statement of my own conviction. But I am not concerned with the effect, I am concerned only with a great and important truth, as it seems to me, and a truth which will, I believe, be curiously, fatefully emphasized in the days near to come, when our Lord shall have taken away His church at His coming in the air.

"Now let me invite your attention to the actual Scriptures which speak of Judas Iscariot. But before doing so let me acknowledge my indebtedness for the *inceptive* thought of all I have said, and shall say, to Dr. Joseph A. Seiss, of Philadelphia, in his wondrous lectures on 'The Revelation.'

"We will turn first again to my text, to the 6th of John, the 70th verse, 'Did I not choose you the twelve, and one of you *is* a devil—*a demon?* He spake of Judas Iscariot.' The second text I want us to note is in John 17, verse 12, and again it is Jesus who makes the solemn declaration: 'Those whom Thou gavest me I have kept, and none of them is lost, but the *Son of Perdition*.' The third text I would draw your attention to is in the 25th verse of Acts 1. It is Peter who is speaking, at the time of the choosing of another as apostle in Judas's place; he says: 'Judas, by transgression, fell, that he might go *to his own place*.' "

In spite of their intentness in the wondrous personality of the messenger, and the extraordinary character of his message, not a few found time to marvel at the facile ease and certainty of touch with which he handled his little pocket Bible, and turned to the desired places. As he finished reading the third passage, and laid the open book down upon the desk, the old hush deepened upon the people.

"Link those three passages together;" he went on, "and you will instantly see what I meant when I said just now, that I believe Judas Iscariot to have been an incarnated demon, and incarnated by the Devil for the one fell purpose of frustrating God's designs for the World's Salvation through Jesus Christ.

"There is not a single recorded good thought, word, or deed that ever Judas thought, said, or did. And do please remember that Christ was never once deceived by him, for in the 64th verse of that 6th of John, we read 'For Jesus knew *from the beginning who* they were that *believed not,* and *who should betray Him.*' And knowing *every*thing, he said of the Betrayer, 'I have chosen—he *is* a demon.' If our Lord had said 'one of you *has* a demon,' the whole statement would have been different, for many, in Christ's days, we find, were possessed by demons, and He, by His divine power cast out the demons. But in Judas we have something different, not a human man in whom a demon has taken up his abode, but a demon who has had a body given him in which to pass among men as a man.

"Christ's statement that he was a *'Son of Perdition,'* is equally damning as to the real nature of Judas Iscariot. He is called the 'son of Simon,' as regards the human side of his life, as Jesus was called 'Joseph's son,'—more especially *Mary's son.*

"But, though, nominally, 'Simon's son,' Judas Iscariot was ever 'a Son of Perdition.' And because he was this —'a demon,' a Son of Perdition, Peter, at Pentecost time, speaking in the Holy Ghost, was able to say that he, Judas, 'went to his *own* place.' We need spend no time in any detailed arguments as to whether this 'place' to which he went in the under-world, was Tartarus or elsewhere, it was *'his own place,' the place of imprisoned demons,* the place where other demons 'who kept not their first estate, but left their own habitation are reserved in chains.' Neither Tartarus or Hell were ever 'prepared' for lost *human* souls, 'but for demons, and, as a demon, Judas went to his *own* place.' "

He paused a moment. His tall, thin form became rigid in the intensity of his service. In the silence, that deepened, the ticking of the clock in the front of the gallery, could be heard plainly in every part of the building.

Slowly he bent his lithe form forward until he leaned far over the Reading Desk. Then stretching out his arm, the long index finger pointing forward, he said:

"Listen, friends! Receive this next part of the message, if you will, if you can. I believe that 'The Man of Sin,' 'The Antichrist,' when he shall be revealed, will be Judas re-incarnated.

"There can be no doubt, I think, but that any one studying Daniel's description of the Anti-christ will realize that, in his *human* personation, he will necessarily be a Jew, for otherwise, the Jews (who will have largely returned to their own land, and will have built their Temple, and resumed their Mosaic service,) would not accept him as their leader, and make their seven years' covenant with him.

"Now, beloved, my last word is a very solemn one. It is this, our Lord's Return for His Bride, the Church, is very near,—'He is even at our doors.' Any day, any hour he may return. We, here, may never reach the point of the 'Benediction' at the *arranged* close of this service, for Jesus may come and call up to Himself everyone of His own in this place. Then what of you here who are not His? For you, there will remain nothing but the horrors of the Tribulation, (should you seek and find God *after* the Translation of the church.)

"Will you be among the Martyrs of the Tribulation, or of the final impenitent, rebels who shall be cast into the Hell reserved for the Devil, for Anti-christ, for the demons; or, blessed thought, will you here and now yield to Christ, and become the saved of the Lord?"

Amid the most intense hush, he added: "Somewhere, even as I have preached of him, and as you have listened, there is, I believe, a young man, of noble stature, exceedingly attractive, wealthy, fascinating,—bewitching, in fact, since 'all the world will wonder after him'—yes, somewhere in the world, perhaps in this very city where we are now gathered, is the young man who, presently, when our Lord has come, when the Church, and the Holy Spirit are gone, will manifest himself as the Anti-christ. May God save everyone of us from *his* reign, for Jesus Christ's sake, Amen!"

A gasping cry of amazed wonder broke from the thousand or more throats. They bowed, as one man, under the silent request of his spread hands, they heard the old, old "Benediction" as they had never heard it before: "May the Grace of our Lord Jesus Christ, the Love of God, and the Fellowship of the Holy Spirit, all unite in leading us into the Peace of God which passeth all understanding, Amen."

Silent, awed, in many cases speechless, the great con-gregation passed out of the several exits of the church. Among them was the woman we know as Judith Mont-marte, and *her son*.

In spite of their pre-occupation, many of the outgoing congregation turned to gaze with wondering eyes upon the handsome young fellow who walked with such a regal air beside his mother, Judith Montmarte. Like Saul, in Israel, he stood a head and shoulders above the tallest of the crowd. And he was magnificently propor-tioned.

On the continent, and in New York and Chicago, Lucien Apleon, was well-known, but only in certain of the *English* circles was he known. Those who knew him, whether men or women, fairly idolized him, in spite of the impenetrable mystery that enveloped his birth.

For a full year Judith Montmarte had disappeared from the ken of the world. Where she went, what she did, what happened to her, none ever knew.

On her re-appearance in her Hungarian home, she called herself Madame Apleon, and her child was Lucien Apleon. No one ever heard of a husband, no one knew the history of that year of disappearance.

Lucien Apleon was now about twenty-five years of age, but with the maturity of face and character of a much older man. He was accounted, by all who knew him, to be the most accomplished man in *everything*, that the world had ever known. The greatest scientists were babes before him. As artist, sculptor, poet, musician, he could not be approached by any living being. And there appeared an almost *creative* power in all he did, since works of every kind of art *grew* under his hand.

Among those who had been in that service, and who turned to look at Lucien Apleon, was Ralph Bastin. It was his last day in London, previous to those years of wandering recorded in "The Twinkling of an Eye."

Often during those years of adventurous wanderings the memory of Ralph Bastin had recalled that wonderful service. One special moment of its recall was during that fateful, sacrificial cave scene in that Carribean Island.

CHAPTER II.

A "SUPER-MAN."

L ONDON was still in its first throes of wonder, speculation, and, in some cases, fearsome dread, at the ever increasing discovery that a number of its citizens had mysteriously disappeared.

"And the most curious part of the whole affair," a prominent London philanthropist had remarked to an informal gathering of the Committee of one of the Great Societies, "is this, that whether we look at the gaps in our own committee, or of any other committee, or of any church—as far as I have been able to gather, the story is the same, the missing people are in almost every case those whom, when they were with us, were least understood by us."

Some such thought had been filling the mind of Ralph Bastin, as he sat in his Editor's chair in the office of the "Courier." Allied to this thought there came another—an almost necessary corollary of the first—namely the new atmosphere of evil, of lawlessness, of wantonness that pervaded the city.

With a jerk, his mind darted backward over the years to that remarkable sermon on Judas and the Antichrist.

"It is true, too true," he murmured, " 'the mystery of iniquity' that has long been working undermining the foundations of all true social and religious safety and solidity, is now to be openly manifested and perfected. The real Christians, the Church of God, which is the

Bride of Christ, has been silently, secretly caught up to
her Lord in the air. She was 'the salt of the earth,' she
kept it from the open putrefaction that has already, now,
begun to work. Thcn, too, that wondrous, silent, but
mighty influence of restraint upon evil.—The Holy
Spirit, Himself, has left the earth, and now, what? All
restraint gone, the world everywhere open to believe the
Antichrist lie, the delusion. The whole tendency of the
teaching, from a myriad pulpits, during the last few
years, has been to prepare the world to receive the
Devil's lie."

For a moment or two he sat in deep thought. Suddenly glancing at the clock, he murmured:

"I wonder what the other papers are saying this
evening."

He rang up his messenger boy on his office phone. The
lad came promptly. Bastin handed him half-a-crown,
saying:

"Get me a copy of the last edition of all the chief
evening papers, Charley, and be smart about it, and
perhaps you will keep the change for your smartness."

In six minutes the lad was back with a sheaf of papers.
Bastin just glanced at them separately, noting the several
times of their issue, then with a "Good boy, Charley!
Keep the change," he unfolded one of the papers.

The boy stood hesitatingly, a moment, then said:
"Beg yer pardin', Mr. Bastin, sir, but wot's yer fink as
people's sayin' 'bout the 'Translation o' the Saints,' as
it's called?"

"I can't say, I am sure, Charley. The careless, and
godless have already said some very foolish things relative to the stupendous event that has just taken place.

and I think, for a few days, they are likely to say even more foolish things. What is the special one that you have heard?"

"Why they sez, sir—its in one o' the *h*eving peepers, they sez—that the people wot's missin' hev been carted off in aeroplanes by some o' the other religionists wot wanted to git rid o' them, an' that the crank religiouses is all gone to——"

"Where?" smiled Bastin.

"I don't think anybody knows where, sir!"

"I do, Charley, and many others to-day, who have been left behind from that great Translation know—they have been 'caught up' into the air where Jesus Christ had come from Heaven to summon them to Himself.

"Mr. Hammond is there, Charley, and that sweet little adopted daughter of mine, whom you once asked me whether 'angels could be more beautiful than she was!'"

"Ah, yus, sir, I recollecks, sir, she wur too bootiful fur words, she wur."

There was one moment's pause, then the boy, with a hurried, "it's all dreadful confuzellin," slipped from the room.

Ralph Bastin opened paper after paper, glanced with the swift, comprehensive eye of the practised journalist at here and there a column or paragraph, and was on the point of tossing the last news-sheet down with the others, on the floor, when his eye caught the wrods, "Joyce, Journalist."

The paragraph recorded the finding of the body of the drunken scoundrel. "From the position of the body," the account read, "and from the nature of the wounds, it would almost seem as though some infernal power had hurled him, head on, against the wall of the room. Whether we believe, or disbelieve the statements concerning the taking away, by some mysterions Translation process, of a number of persons from our midst, yet the fact remains that each hour is marked by the finding of some poor dead creature, under circumstances quite as tragically mysterious as this case of Joyce the reporter."

For a time Ralph Bastin sat deep in thought. He had not yet written the article for to-morrow's issue "From the Prophet's chair." He felt his insufficiency, he realized the need of being God's true witness in this hour that was ushering in the awful reign of The Antichrist. He did the *best* thing, he knelt in prayer, crying:

"O God, I am so ignorant, teach me, give me Thy wisdom in this momentous hour. If those who cleave to Thee amid this awful time must seal their witness with death, must face martyrdom, then let me be counted worthy to die for Thee. In the old days, before yesterday's great event, all prayer had to be offered to Thee through Jesus Christ. I know no other way, please then hear my prayer, and accept it, for Jesus Christ's sake. Amen."

Rising from his knees, with a sense of solemn calm pervading all his soul, he presently took his pen and began to write rapidly, his mind seeming, to him, to be consciously under the domination of the divine.

Embodying the various items over which he had so recently mused, as to the awfulness of the development of evil that would increasingly mark the near coming days, now that all restraints were taken away, he went on to show that now that the Devil, who had, for ages, been the Prince of the Power of the air, with all his foul following of demons, had been cast down out of that upper realm, where Christ and his translated saints had taken up their abode, the forces of evil upon the earth would be magnified and multiplied a million-fold.

"Christ and the Devil," he went on, "never can dwell in the same realm, hence the coming of Christ into the air meant the descent to earth, of the Devil and, with him all the invisible hosts of evil. The wildest, weirdest imagination could not conceive all the horrors that must come upon those who presently will refuse to wear the 'Mark of the Beast' and bow to worship him."

Suddenly, at this point in his writing, a curious sense of some presence, other than his own, came over him, and slowly, almost reluctantly he looked up.

He started visibly, for, seated in the chair on the opposite side of his desk, was a visitor. The man was the most magnificent specimen of the human race he had ever seen, a giant, almost, in stature, handsome to a degree, and with a certain regal air about him.

Bastin had involuntarily leaped to his feet, and now stammered:

"I—er—beg pardon, but I did not hear you come in."

Even as he spoke two things happened. His mind swept backward over the years to the day of that wonderful Judas sermon he had heard, and with this recalled memory there came the recollection of his turning to look into the face of that magnificent looking young man who had been the cynosure of all eyes as he left the church with his mother. He was conscious also of a strange uncanny sense that this smiling handsome man, with mocking, dancing light in his eyes, was no ordinary man.

In that same instant, too, Ralph Bastin knew who his visitor was, since he had become familiarized by the illustrated papers and magazines, with the features of "The Genius of the Age"—as he was often styled— Lucien Apleon.

"My name," said the smiling visitor, "is Lucien Apleon. As editor of a great journal like the 'Courier,' you know who I am when you know my name, even though we have never met before. You were so busy, so absorbed, when I came in that I did not so much as cough to announce my presence."

Ralph longed to ask him if he came through the door, or how, since he had heard no sound. But he did not put his question, but replied:

"Who has not heard and read of Lucien Apleon, 'The Genius of the Age,' sage, savant, artist, sculptor, poet, novelist, a giant in intellect, the Napoleon of commercial capacity, the crœsus for wealth, and master of all courts and diplomacy. But I had not heard that you were in England, the last news *par'* of you which I read, gave you as at that wonderful city, the New Babylon, more wonderful, I hear, than any of the former cities of its name and site."

Ralph had talked more than he needed to have done, but he wanted time to recover his mental balance, for his nerves had been considerably startled by the suddenness, the uncanniness of his visitor's appearance.

There was a curious quizzical, mocking look in the eyes of Apleon while Ralph was speaking. The latter noted it and had an uncomfortable consciousness that the mocking-eyed visitor was reading him like a book.

"I only landed to-day," replied Apleon.

"Steamer?" asked Ralph.

"No, by a new aerial type of my own invention," replied Apleon. "It brought me from Babylon to London in about as many minutes as it would have occupied the best aeronaut, days, by the best machines of a year ago."

He laughed. There was a curious sound in the laugh, it was mocking yet musical, it was eerie yet merry. Involuntarily Ralph thought of Grieg's "Dance of the Imps," and Auber's overture "Le Domino Noir."

"But I have not yet explained my object in calling upon you," the visitor went on. "I have, of course, seen this morning's 'Courier,' and have been intensely interested, and, will you mind, if I say it, amused."

"Amused, Mr. Apleon?" cried Ralph.

"Yes, intensely amused," went on the mocking-eyed visitor. "I do not mean with the issue as regards its *general* contents, it was to the 'Prophet's Chair' column that I alluded."

Ralph, regarding him questioningly, inclined his head, without speaking.

"Do you really believe, Mr. Bastin," went on the visitor, "what you have written in that column? Do you really believe that a certain section of Christians, out of every one of the visible Evangelical churches of this land, and elsewhere, have been translated into the air? That the Holy Spirit of the Christian New Testament, the third Person of the Trinity, whom that same New Testament declares was sent to the earth when the Nazarene Christ went home to His Father—please, note, Mr. Bastin, that I am using the terms of the orthodox Christian, though I tell you frankly I do not believe a word of the jumble which, for nearly two thousand years, has been accepted as a divinely inspired Revelation to so-called fallen man?"

"Yes," replied Ralph, and his voice rang with a rare assurance, and every line of his face held a wondrous nobility. "Yes, I believe it all. If I had not been a blind, conceited fool of a sinner, a week ago, I should have known that all this, and much more was true, and I should have found my way in penitence and faith to the feet of the Nazarene, of Jesus Christ the World's Redeemer, and, finding pardon for my sin, as I should have done, I should have been made one of the Church of God, as my friend, and Editor-in-chief, Tom Hammond, had done. And, had I listened to him, I should now have been with those blessed translated ones of whom I have written in that article of which you speak, Mr. Apleon.

"I sat in that chair where you now sit," Ralph went on. "Mr. Hammond, in his eagerness to win me to Christ, leant forward over this desk—he was sitting where I am—to lay his hand on my wrist, when, with angry impatience, I leaped to my feet, and declaring that he must be going out of his head, I swung round on my heel.

"Instantly there fell upon the room an eerie stillness. I swung back on my heel to reply to my friend, but his chair was empty, he was gone—gone to the Christ whom he loved, 'caught up in the air' to meet his Lord, where all those other missing saints have been taken.

"Yes, yes, Mr. Apleon, a thousand times yes, to your question, 'do I believe all that I have written there in that article.' Here in this little pamphlet—" He laid his hand, as he spoke, upon a small book that had been Tom Hammond's, which bore the title "THE SECOND COMING OF OUR LORD JESUS CHRIST. Systematically arranged from passages in the Holy Scriptures, for Students, Teachers, and others. By the Rev. Robert Middleton."

"Here, in this little book," he went on, "there is not only set out with the most luminous clearness, with the actual Bible texts, all that I have written in that article, but also many other truths and texts which have already been literally fulfilled during the last forty-eight hours—even as the book said that they would be."

With the old mocking, quizzical smile, the handsome Apleon interrupted him, asking,:

"What do you mean by the *real* Church of God? The Romish Church, The Greek Church, The Anglican Church or any one of the multitude of dissenting churches?"

It was Ralph's turn to smile now, as he said:

"None of those churches could be called THE CHURCH OF GOD. The *true,* the *real* church was composed of true believers, men and women who had been born again by the Spirit of God, and who, numbered among every section of so-called Christians—and some who were wholly unattached—made up in their wide-world entirety the true Church of God, the Bride of Christ."

"And what," asked Apleon, "of the rest, the vast bulk of the worshippers at the various churches? What is their fate to be?"

"God only knows!" replied Bastin. "Some, at least, have already sought, and found God, or believe they have, even as I have sought, and believe that I have found God. But the vast bulk of the people already seem to be rollicking in a curious sense of non-restraint. I remember some years ago, hearing a lady say that visiting the houses of one of the worst streets in Winchester, and speaking to the people as to their eternal welfare, she found one woman particularly hardened.

To this woman she said: 'But, my dear sister, think of what it will be to be eternally lost, to be separated from God, and from all that is pure and good, for ever, and in a state and place which the Bible calls Hell.' And the woman laughed, as she said: 'Well, there's one thing, I shall not be lonely there, for I shall have all my neighbours around me, for every one in this street is on the same track as me.' "

A sardonic smile curled the full lips of Apleon, as ne said:

"Poor deluded soul! For if there is such a place as that Hell, that underworld of lost souls of which your Bible speaks, and declares that it was prepared for the Devil and his angels, and that woman and her neighbours find themselves there, they will realize that hell, for its lost, is the loneliest spot in the universe, since each soul will hate the other and will live alone, apart in its own hideous realm of anguish and remorse."

Lifting his eyes to his visitor's face, as the latter delivered himself to this strange speech, Bastin was startled to note the expression on the handsome face. The eyes, unutterably sad for one instant, turned suddenly to savage hate, the mouth was as cruel as death, the eyes grew baleful, like the eyes of a snake that is being whipped to death.

He was startled even more by the tones of his voice when he said:

"And what of the Anti-christ of whom you have spoken and written? Do you believe what you have written?"

"I most certainly do," replied Ralph.

Again the sardonic smile filled all Apleon's face as he returned:

"Then if all that you say and write be true, as regards the coming Anti-christ, and you continue to wear the late editor's mantle when you write 'The Prophet's chair' articles, how long do you suppose that that powerful *super*-man, the Anti-christ of your belief, will let you alone. If he is to be so powerful, and if the devil is to energize him, as you say;—even as you profess to believe that he has called into being—is now actually dwelling on the earth, though invisible, and all his angels (demons, I believe they are called in the Bible) are moving about invisibly among the people on the earth, among the people of this wonderful London, if all this, I say, be so, how long do you suppose you will be allowed, by his Satanic Majesty, to ply your trade of warner of the peoples? Why, man, your life is not worth the snap of a finger?"

Ralph smiled. The smile transfigured his face, even as the same sort of smile transfigured the faces of the martyrs of old time, beginning with Stephen.

"I care not how long I live," he replied. "The only care I have now is to be true to my convictions, true to my God."

The telephone rang at that instant. "Excuse me one moment, Mr. Apleon," he said, turning to the instrument.

There followed a few moments exchanges on the 'phone, then replacing the receiver he turned. But his visitor was gone.

"That's curious!" he muttered. "I did not hear a sound of his going, any more than I did of his coming. Uncanny, eerie, creepy, almost!"

There was a tap at the door. "Come in!" he called.

The messenger boy, Charley, entered with a sheaf of proof galleys.

"Did you see that tall gentleman pass out, Charley?" he asked. "Did he go down stairs, or into one of the other offices?"

"Tall gennelman, sir? There aint bin no one come along this way, sir, nobody couldn't pass my little hutch wivout me a seein' on 'em. I ain't been out no wheres, an' I knows no one aint come by—least ways, not this way, not past my place."

"If any tall gentleman does come up, Charley, show him in to me, at once please."

Ralph had had time, during Charley's extended answer, to recover himself from the amaze that the boy's first sentence has produced in him.

"That's all, Charley!" he added, turning to his desk.

The boy gave him a curious, puzzled look, lingered for the fraction of a second, then slowly turned and left the office.

When the door had closed behind him, Ralph, who had *felt* all that had passed in that moment of the boy's hesitancy, though he had purposely refrained from looking up, lifted his head and glanced around him.

"If I did not know better," he murmured, "I should suppose that the whole incident was but a dream, or hallucination."

A perplexed look filled his face, as he continued: "What does it all mean?"

Again, in a flash, the memory of that Judas sermon swept back over him, and the startling statement recurred to him "Somewhere, even as I have preached of him, and as you have listened, there is, I believe, a young man of noble stature, exceedingly attractive,

wealthy, fascinating, bewitching in fact, since 'all the
world will wonder after him'—yes, somewhere in the
world, perhaps in this very city where we are now gathered, is the young man who, presently, when our Lord
has come, when the Church, and the Holy Spirit are
gone, will manifest himself as the Anti-christ."

Coming back at this particular moment, Ralph asked
himself: "Is Lucien Apleon the Anti-christ?"

He paused an instant, then, as a sudden startling sense
of assurance of the fact swept into his soul he cried:

"He is! I have seen the Anti-christ!"

For nearly an hour he sat on his chair, his mind
wrapped in deep thought, and occasionally referring to
a book of prophecy which Tom Hammond had evidently
deeply studied.

At the end of the hour, he bowed his head upon his
hands, and held silent communion with God, seeking
wisdom to write and speak and live the Truth.

CHAPTER III

"TO THE WORLD, THE FLESH, AND THE DEVIL"

THE next day was Sunday. It was also the first Sunday of the month. As he bathed and dressed, Ralph found himself wondering whether the churches and chapels would be filled, whether the awe and fear that had fallen upon so many Christian professors during the first hours after the "Rapture," would drive them to the churches.

"The first of the month," he mused. "The Lord's Supper has been the order of the day in most places. I wonder if it will be celebrated to-day?"

Until He come!" he mused on. "He *has* come, so that the Lord's Supper, as part of the worship of the churches is concerned, can have no further meaning. Will any attempt be made to celebrate it, to-day, I wonder?"

Every available moment of the fateful week that had just passed he had occupied in deep reading the prophetic scriptures referring to The Coming of the Lord, and the events which follow. He had also studied deeply every book on the subject which he could secure, that was likely to help him to understand the position of affairs. Again and again, he had said to himself: "How could I have been such a fool? a journalist, a bookman, a lover of research, professing to have the open mind which should be the condition of every man of my trade, and yet never to have studied my Bible, never to have sought to know what all the startling events of the past decade.

pointed to. Surely, surely, Tom Carlyle was right about we British—'mostly fools.' '

At breakfast he ate and drank only sufficient to satisfy the sense of need. Previous to "The Rapture" he had been a bit of an Epicure, now he scarcely noted what he ate or drank.

Almost directly his meal was finished, he left the house. The journalistic instinct was strong enough within him to make him desire to see what changes, if any, would be apparent in London on this first Sunday after the momentous event that had so recently come upon the world.

Turning out of the quiet square where his lodgings were, he was instantly struck by a new tone in the streets. There was an utter absence of the old-time "Sabbath" sense.

The gutterways were already lined with fruit and other hawkers, their coarse voices, crying their wares, making hideous what should have been a Sunday quiet

It was barely ten, yet already many of the Tea Rooms were open, and most of them seemed thronged, whole families, and pleasure-parties taking breakfast, evidently.

He passed a large and popular theatre, across the whole front of which was a huge, hand-painted announcement, "Matinee at 2, this afternoon. Performance to-night 7-45. New Topical song entitled "The Rapture," on the great event of the week. Living Pictures at both performances: "The Flight of the Saints."

Ralph, in his amaze, had paused to read the full contents of the announcement. He shuddered as he took in the full import of the blasphemy. Surveying the crowd that stood around the notice, he was struck by the composition of the little mob. It was anything but a *low-*

class crowd. Many of them were evidently of the upper middle class, well-dressed, and often intellectual-looking people.

He was turning to leave the spot, when a horsey-looking young fellow close to him, in a voice loud enough to be heard by the whole crowd—he evidently meant that it should—cried:

"Well, if it's true that all the long-faced puritans have been carted off, vamoused, kidnapped, "Rapturized," as they call it, and that now there's to be no Theatre Censor, and every one can do as they like, well then, good riddance to the kill-joys, I say."

"And so say all of us," sang a voice, almost everyone present joining in the song.

When twenty yards off Ralph could hear the blasphemy ringing out "The Devil's a jolly good fellow, and so say all of us!"

"What will London be like in a month's time!" he mused.

He moved on quickly, but even as he went the thought thrust itself upon him, that half London, for some reason or the other, was abroad in the streets unusually early. His own objective was a great Nonconformist church, where one of London's most popular and remarkable preachers had ministered. He had been one of the comparatively few whose ministry had been characterized by a close adherence to the Word of God, and an occasional solemn word of expository warning and exhortation *anent* the "Coming of the Lord."

Ralph was within a stone's throw of the great building when the squeaking tones of Punchinello, reached his ears, while a deep roar of many laughing voices accompanied the squeakings. A moment more and he was abreast of a crowd of many hundreds of people gathered around the Punch and Judy show.

Sick in soul at all that told of open blasphemy everywhere around him, he hurried on, not so much as casting an eye at the show, though it was impossible for him to miss the question and answer that rang out from the show.

"Now, now Mr. Punch, where's your poor wife? Have you done away with her?"

"No," screamed the hook-nosed puppet, "Not me, I aint done away with her, she done away with herself, she's gone and got 'Rapturized.' "

Then, above the ribald laughter of the crowd, the squeaking puppet sang:

> "Oh, p'raps she is, p'raps she aint,
>   An' p'raps she's gone to sea,
> Or p'raps she's gone to Brigham Young
>   A Mormonite to be."

Ralph shivered as with chill, as he went up the steps of the great church to which he had been aiming. It was filling fast. Five minutes after he entered, the doors had to be closed, there was not even standing room.

He swept the huge densely-packed building with his keen eyes. Many present were evidently accustomed to gather there, though the bulk were curious strangers. A strange hush was upon the people, a half-frightened look upon many faces, and a general air of suspense.

Once, someone in the gallery cracked a nut. The sound was almost as startling as a pistol shot, and hundreds of faces were turned in the direction of the sound.

Ralph noticed that the Communion table, on the lower platform under the rostrum was covered with white, and evidently arranged as for the Lord's Supper.

Exactly at eleven, someone emerged from a vestry and passed up the rostrum stairs. A moment later the man was standing at the desk. Many instantly recognized him. It was the Secretary of the Church.

A dead hush fell upon the people.

The face of the man was deathly pale, his eyes were dull and sunken. Twice his lips parted and he essayed to speak, but no sound escaped him. The hush deepened.

Then, at last, low and husky came the words "My dear friends—for I recognize some who have been wont to gather here on the Sundays, though the majority are strangers, I think."

His eyes slowly swept the great congregation. "We have, I believe, many of us, gathered here this morning more by a new, strange, common instinct, than by mere force of Sunday habit. Yet, I cannot but think that many of us, solemnized by the events that have transpired since last Sunday, have met more in the Spirit of real seeking after God than ever we have done before."

A few voices joined in a murmur of assent, but something like a ripple of mocking laughter came from others. And one voice in the gallery laughed outright— it was the man who had cracked the nut.

Momentarily unnerved by that laughter the speaker paused. Then recovering himself he went on:

"Our pastor has gone; the Puritans (as we were wont to call them) are gone; and we know now—now that it is too late for those of us who are 'left'—that they have been 'caught up' into the air, to be with their Lord forever."

He glanced down at the white-draped communion table, as he continued:

"Our church officer has performed his usual monthly office, and has spread the Table for the Lord's Supper, but it dawns upon us, friends, how useless, how empty is the symbol since it was only ordained 'until He should come.' He has come, and we, the unready, have been left behind."

"Tommy Rot!"

The expression came angrily, sneeringly from the man in the gallery, the man who cracked that nut, and who had laughed so boisterously a moment ago.

Many eyes were turned up to the man, but no voice of reprimand came, no cry of "shame!" or of "Turn him out," was raised.

All that had happened during the days of the past week, had served to fill many of the people gathered there that morning, with a curious mingling of doubt, hesitancy, fearsomeness, and uncertainty, as well as an unconscious growth of a new strange skepticism, and a carelessness that almost amounted to recklessness.

"As it is with many more here, this morning," the Secretary went on, "some members of my family have gone, been caught up—"

"Aviated!" laughed a ribald voice, and this time it came from another part of the building.

Disregarding the interruption, the secretary went on:

"My wife has gone—" His voice shook with the deep emotion that stirred him, and for a moment he was too moved to speak. Then recovering himself with an effort he continued:

"My daughter, too, who against my wish had offered herself as a Foreign Missionary, has gone. Both wife and daughter lived in the spirit of expectancy of the Coming of Christ into the air. Now they are with Him, to be with Him for ever."

The ribald voice that had last interrupted, again broke into the Secretary's touching words. This time the interrupter roared out a stanza or two of a wretched song:

"Will no one tell me where they're gone,
My bursting heart with grief is torn,
I wish I never had been born,
    I've lost, I've lost my vife."

A hundred or more voices roared with laughter. The devil of blasphemy was growing bolder.

But in the silence that immediately followed the laughter, the Secretary went on again:

"I have been a deeply *religious* man, even as Nicodemus and Paul were, before their conversion. But now that it is too late to share in the bliss of the glorious Translation, I have discovered that Religion, without Christ, without the Regeneration of the New Birth, is evidently useless, otherwise, I, with scores of others in this church, this morning, who have, for years, listened to a full-orbed gospel from our God-filled translated pastor, would be now with those of our loved ones who have 'ascended up on high.'"

He paused for the briefest fraction of a second, a look of keenest anguish filled his face, his eyes grew moist with unshed tears, and were full of appeal, of enquiry, as he swept the great assembly, crying:

"There must be thousands upon thousands left in our land, who, like myself, deceived themselves, and thus, unwittingly deceived others, and in whose souls there rises the cry: 'How can we find God? Who will show us the way?'

"Friends, I have searched my New Testament from end to end. I have been up two whole nights, and I have read the New Testament through from Matthew to Revelation, twice. But I can find no provision for the position I find myself in. I can find no guidance as to *how* to be saved. The whole situation is too solemn, too awful for any fooling. Does anyone here know? Can anyone here tell us how we may find God, now that the salt of the earth—the real Christians are gone, and now, too, that the Holy Spirit who, of old time—not yet a full week, but it seems an eternity—led souls to God through Christ."

There was something so solemn, so pathetic in the man's manner and utterance, that even the ribald fools who had previously interrupted, were silent.

The hush was intense. The ticking of the clock could be heard distinctly.

Impelled by a power which he could not have defined or described, Ralph Bastin rose to his feet.

The hush deepened. Then a voice broke the silence, crying:

"Bastin, editor of 'The Courier'!"

He was very pale, but the light of a rare courage flashed in his eyes. He acknowledged the recognition of himself by an inclination of the head. Then amid a strange hush he began to speak, his voice husky, at first, rapidly clearing as he went on:

"Friends, I take it that this is the most momentous Sunday that has ever been, since the first one—the day of the resurrection of the Christ. Our friend who has just spoken has surely voiced the question of many hearts here this morning, and many other troubled hearts the wide world over.

"Let me say, right here, that my friend and colleague, Mr. Tom Hammond, the originator and late editor of 'The Courier,' was in the very act of explaining the wonderful, expected return of Christ (expected by him though scoffed at by myself) when he was 'caught up' from my very presence, and then I knew what a fool I had been to neglect God and His salvation."

The nut-cracking interrupter in the gallery, with a burst of laughter, began mockingly to sing the old revival chorus, "Come to Jesus, come to Jesus, come to Jesus, just now, just——"

"Silence! you blasphemous, ribald fool!" The words leaped from the lips of Ralph Bastin, in a tone of command that literally awed the interrupter. The effect, too, upon the hesitating, vacillating mass of people was, for the moment at least, to arouse their sympathy with Ralph, and a little murmur of applause followed.

At the same time a soldier in uniform, a man of giant proportions, who was sitting almost immediately behind the disturber, rose in his seat, and addressing the man in front of him, cried, in a stentorian voice:

"See here, mouthy, we're about fed up with your gas, so if you give us so much as one wag of that cursed red rag of yours, I'll pick you up and snap you in half across my knee, as I would snap a stick."

This time the applause broke out all over the crowded church. When it ceased, Ralph standing straight as a larch, and looking up at the soldier, gave a military salute, as he said: "Thank you, brave soldier."

Coming back to his audience, he went on, as if there had been no interruption:

"I, too, like the gentleman who addressed us just now, have read the whole of the Bible through, and the New Testament *twice,* and I can find no *definite* provision or Revelation for those who are left behind—that is as to the *how,* I mean, of salvation. Yet that there are to be many saved during the next seven years, is evident, since there is to be a great multitude come out of *The Great* Tribulation, and thousands of these will be martyrs for God, refusing to wear the Mark of the Beast.

"In one of the pamphlets I have been studying on 'The second coming of the Lord,' I have found this statement, that Christ, during His ministry, preached the Gospel *of the Kingdom,* which is explained as referring to the fact that, as a Jew, as the Messiah, He came to His own people the Jews, the chosen *earthly* people of God, and that if they would have accepted Him as their Messiah, His Kingdom—with Himself reigning as King—might have been set up there and then. But they rejected Him, yes, even when Peter, at Pentecost, after the Ascension of Christ, made the final offer in those wonderful words of his.

"As a nation, they rejected Him, rejected their Lord and King, and henceforth, until He should come again. (He came last week, as we know, now that it is too late for us to share in the glory of that coming.) Until that coming, as I said, the Gospel to be preached was to be the 'Gospel of the Grace of God,' and not the 'Gospel of the Kingdom.' 'The Gospel of the Grace of God,' included all peoples, Gentile as well as Jew, while 'the Gospel of the Kingdom,' in its first preaching, was especially a message to the Jew.

"Now, friends, since there appears to be no *special* Revelation left as to how men and women are to be saved, I have been forced to the conclusion that we must go back to the Old Testament word: 'Seek ye the Lord' —'Call upon the Name of the Lord'—'Trust ye in the Lord'—'Come now and let us reason, saith the Lord. Though your sins be as scarlet, they shall be as white as snow, though they be red like crimson, they shall be as wool.' 'The Lord is nigh unto them who are of broken heart, and *saveth* such as be of a *Contrite* spirit.'

"I have taken my own stand upon this, that God, the God of the Old Testament, is the same God, who pities like a father, and that if we confess our sin, and witness a true confession, He will forgive us our sin, and though we can never be part of that wondrous *Bride* of Christ, whom, last week He caught up to Himself into the Heavenlies, yet we may be eternally saved. And, friends, whether I am right or wrong, I am daily pleading the Name of Jesus Christ in all my approaches to God. I plead the Blood of Jesus Christ, and the power of that Blood, to save me; for, as far as I understand myself, in this matter, my belief, my trust is the same as that which inspired the saints who were translated at the 'Rapture'—as that event has come to be called.

"In my studies during the past week—would God I had been wise, and given myself to all this a month ago, I should then have shared in the glory of that Rapturous event of which all our minds are so full.

"But, as I was saying, in my studies during the past week, I have seen that in Revelation Seven, in the account of those who are to be saved *during* the seven years of the present dispensation, (and which has just begun) that they 'have washed their robes and made them white *in the blood of the Lamb.*' So that though I am not able to reduce my standing to an actual theological position—statement—yet I pin my soul, my faith on the Eternal character of God, and on the efficacy of the Blood of Jesus, as shown in Revelation Seven, fourteen."

He paused for an instant, and his eyes swept the great assembly sorrowfully, sadly, as he went on:

"But it is forced upon me that what is done by us, in this matter of seeking God, must be done by us *now, at once.* Every hour increases the danger of delay because the powers of evil, of the Antichrist, are already growing more and more rampant, more and more pronounced. Presently, friends, we know not but that any hour or even moment now, the awful delusion of the Antichrist lie, may be actually formulated into speech and print, and it will be so almost universally absorbed by mankind, and its influence be so pervading, so saturating, in every class, of society, that it will every hour become harder, more difficult for the individual soul to turn to God."

He paused again for one instant. Then startlingly, suddenly, the words "Great God!" leaped from his lips. They sounded like a mighty sob.

"Great God!" he repeated with an anguish that awed the people. "The great mass of people in London, are already mocking God. They laugh at the notion of there being a God, of there being any Retribution. The great mass of the people are ripe for anything, even for a public, official denial of the very existence of God. Deluded, they will believe any lie, THE FOUL LIE.

"How long is it since, in France, in the Revolution, the leading men, the 'flower' of that capricious nation, carried in triumph in grand procession the most beautiful harlot of Paris, to the Cathedral of Notre Dame, and,

unveiling and kissing her before the high altar, proclaimed her as the 'Goddess of Reason,' exhorting the
multitude of people to forget all the childish things that
they had been taught as to the thunders of the wrath of
God, for God was not, and had never been.

"And all that happened while the 'salt of the earth,'
was abroad, and while that great, divine restrainer of
evil, the Holy Spirit, the third Person of the Trinity,
was still upon the earth exercising His restraint.

"And, in a week from to-day, I believe it will be
absolutely impossible to get a gathering like this. The
world, the Flesh, the Devil, the Antichrist, will have
almost absolute sway, and if any of us will live to God,
we must be prepared to suffer the direst persecution, and
all the horrors of the Great Tribulation, with its thousands of martyrs, will be the portion of those who will
cleave to God, and flout Antichrist."

A deep, sullen growl, like that of some huge savage
beast, rose here and there from a number of dissenters
to these predictions.

Ralph lifted his head proudly, and fearlessly for his
God, as he cried:

"There rises the first growl of the slumbering demon
of Antichrist, which, only too soon, shall possess almost
the whole world. Soon, a year, or two, less than that,
doubtless, Antichrist will dominate the earth's peoples.
None will be able to trade, to buy or sell, unless they
bear on their forehead or their *right* hand, the Mark of
the Beast. What will that mark be? I cannot tell. I do
not know, no one save Antichrist, and the Devil who has
incarnated him, can as yet know, I think."

Again that growl rose from the throats of some of
the listeners. This time it was deeper, fuller. more voices

joined in it, and the savage note was more pronounced.

Suddenly, a mighty roar of thousands of voices, mingled with the blare of brass instruments penetrated into the building from the street. There followed, instantly, a general rising to their feet, and a rush of the people to the exits. The crush at the exits was terrible. Screams of women mingled with the hoarse cursings of men—men who had never uttered an oath before, found their mouth filled with hideous, blasphemous oaths. It was as if the very devil himself had suddenly possessed the crowd.

Ralph found himself alongside the Secretary of the church, the man who had preceded him in speaking. The pair watched and listened for a moment while noisily, slowly, painfully the people passed out of the building.

Involuntarily there sprang to Ralph's lips, and, before he realized it, he was uttering the words:

"The whole herd ran violently down a steep place into the sea, and was choked."

The two men were strangers, yet as they turned and faced each other, by some common impulse they clasped hands. For one instant it looked as though each would have spoken. Then, as though some strange power had tied their tongues, they moved on silently, side by side, down the wide aisle of the church, and passed out through the entrance doors of the now empty building.

The streets were filled with surging masses of people, and there was a glare of ruddy flames, while dense volumes of smoke poured into the upper air from the first of two huge cars drawn by hundreds of excited men, boys, and even women and girls.

In the center of the platform of the first car was a huge, altar-like construction in polished iron or steel.

The center of the altar was evidently a deep hollow cauldron, into which a score of men, costumed as satyrs, were pitchforking Bibles. The four sides of the Altar-cauldron had open bars, so that, fanned on every side by the double draught of the car's motion, and the fairly stiff breeze that was blowing, the furnace roared fiercely, fed, as it incessantly was by the copies of God's Word.

Hundreds of wildly-excited men and women—many seemed semi-drunken—attired in every conceivable grotesqueness of costume, and forming a kind of open-air fancy-dress ball, disported themselves shamelessly about the cauldron car, and the triumphal car that followed in its wake.

The latter was a gorgeous structure, finished in gold, purple, and imitation white marble. Its center was a kind of *tableaux vivant*. On one side was an effigy of a parsonic kind of man, crucified head downwards upon a cross. A second side showed a theatre front with a staring announcement *"seven* day performances." A third side showed a figure of "Bacchus" crowned with vine-leaves and grape-bunches. A fourth side showed an entrance to a Law Court, with an announcement: "Closed Eternally, for since there is no marriage, there is no divorce."

Above all this was a golden throne, and in a deep purple-plush-covered chair sat a florid, coarsely-beautiful woman, with long hair of golden hue hanging down upon her shoulders and blowing in the breeze. She was literally naked, save for a ruffle of pink muslin about her waist. Upon her head was a crown, in her right hand she held a gilded crozier.

The most wanton, hideous licentiousness was the

order of the hour among the mob of fancy-costumed people.

Ralph Bastin and his companion followed in the wake of the foaming, raging sea of semi-mad people.

"The French Revolution business over again," said Ralph—he had to shout into his friend's ear to be heard.

His companion nodded an assent, then bawled back:

"Whither are they bound, I wonder?"

Ralph pointed to a banner bearing the inscription, "To St. Pauls."

The procession swept on, and seven minutes later the cars were rounded up in front of the open space before the Cathedral.

A score of policemen had managed to muster on the upper step of the flight. But the rush of the mob was irresistible. They took entire possession of the steps and all the open space around even to the head of Ludgate Hill.

Ralph had got separated from his companion, and found himself swept close up to the great triumphal car. Above him seated smilingly on her purple throne, in all her shameless nakedness, was the beautiful form of the foul souled harlot. Her gilded crozier was upheld between her naked knees, and now, in her right hand she held a goblet of champagne, just passed up to her.

A bugle sounded for silence. The hush was instantaneous. Then as she held the goblet high aloft, her clear, shrill voice rang out in the toast she gave:

"To the World, the Flesh, and the Devil!"

She drained the sparkling draught, and tossed the goblet down into the upraised hand of a handsome, but dissolute-looking man, who, attired in the theatrical idea of Mephistopheles, appeared to be a kind of Master of Ceremonies.

A mighty roar of applause, mingled with cries of "Dolly Durden! Dear little Dolly Durden!" accompanied the drinking of the toast.

Again the bugle rang out for silence, and amid a hush as before, Mephistopheles shouted:

"The Sunday of the Puritans is dead and *damned!* Their Bible is burned and a dead letter!"

He pointed, as he uttered the last sentence, to the Satyrs who were piling the last of their stock of Bibles into the fiery furnace of the cauldron-altar.

His blasphemies were greeted with a roar of applause. Then, as he obtained a comparative silence by the raising of his hand, he yelled:

"To Hyde Park."

The band struck up "Good St. Anthony," and the monster procession, swept down Ludgate Hill, hundreds of throats belching out the words of the song, to the music of the band:

> "St. Anthony sat on a lowly stool,
>   A large black book he held in his hand,
> Never his eyes from the page he took,
>   With steadfast soul the page he scanned.
> The Devil was in his best humour that day,
>   That ever his Highness was known to be in,—
> That's why he sent out his imps to play
>   With sulphur, and tar, and pitch, and resin:
> They came to the saint in a motley crew,
>   Twisted and twirl'd themselves about,—
> Imps of every shape and hue,
>   A devilish, strange, and rum-looking rout.
> Yet the good St. Anthony kept his eyes
>   So firmly fixed upon his book,
> Shouts nor laughter, sighs nor cries,
>   Never could win away his look."

Verse after verse belched forth from the now more or
less raucous throats of the blasphemous mob, until,
with unholy unctiousness, reaching the last verse but one,
they screamed laughingly, vilely:

> "A thing with horny eyes was there—
>   With horny eyes just like the dead,
> While fish-bones grew instead of hair
>   Upon his bald and skinless head.
> Last came an imp—how unlike the rest,—
>   A lovely-looking female form,
> And while with a whisper his cheek she press'd,
>   Her lips felt downy, soft, and warm;
> As over his shoulder she bent, the light
>   Of her brilliant eyes upon his page
> Soon filled his soul with mild delight,
>   And the good old chap forgot his age.
> And the good St. Anthony boggled his eyes
>   So quickly o'er his old black book,—
> Ho! Ho! at the corners they 'gan to rise,
>   And he couldn't choose but have a look.
>
> "There are many devils that walk this world,
>   Devils so meagre and devils so stout,
> Devils that go with their tails uncurl'd,
>   Devils with horns and devils without.
> Serious devils, laughing devils,
>   Devils black and devils white,
> Devils uncouth, and devils polite.
>   Devils for churches, devils for revels,
> Devils with feathers, devils with scales,
>   Devils with blue and warty skins,
> Devils with claws like iron nails,
>   Devils with fishes' gills and fins;
> Devils foolish, devils wise,
>   Devils great, and devils small,—
> But a laughing woman with two bright eyes
>   Proves to be the worst devil of them all."

It was all of Hell, Hellish, and should have proved
conclusively, if proof had been desired, that with the
translation of the Church, and the flight of the Holy
Spirit, the last restraint upon man's natural love of
lawlessness had been taken away.

Sweeping westwards, the hideous, blasphemous procession was continually augmented by crowds that swarmed up from side-streets, and fell-in in the rear of the marching throng.

Somewhere on the route, owing to a kind of backwash of the surging people, Ralph Bastin and the Secretary of the Church had become separated. At Picadilly circus they came suddenly face to face again.

"What is this foul, blasphemous movement? What does it mean?" asked the Secretary. "Is this a beginning of *organized* lawlessness on the part of the Anti-christ?"

"I think not," replied Ralph. "I should rather say that it was a bit of wanton outrage of all the decencies of ordinary life, and arranged by some of the rude fellows—male and female—of the baser sort. You noticed, of course, that most of those immediately connected with the two cars, looked like the drinking, smoking, sporting fellows who are the *habitues* of the music-halls and the promenades of the theatres."

An uproarious cheering of the mighty throng interrupted Ralph for a moment. Only those well to the front of the procession could know the cause of the cheering, but the whole mass of people joined in it. As the roar died away, Ralph Bastin took up the broken thread of his reply:

"Yet, for all I have just said, I feel it in my bones as Mrs. Beecher Stowe's old negress 'mammy' used to say, that this foul demonstration on this golden Sunday morning, is the unauthorized unofficial beginning of the Antichrist movement."

There was a couple of hundred yards between the tail of the actual procession, and Ralph and his companion. Hundreds of people thronged the sidewalks, but the road was fairly clear, and along the gutter-way there swept a gang of boys with coarse, raucous laughter, kicking—football fashion—two or three of the half-burned Bibles that had fallen from the cauldron-altar on the car.

The church Secretary visibly shuddered at the sacrilege. A pained look shot into Ralph Bastin's face, as he said:

"Such wanton, open sacrilege as that could only have become possible by the gradual decay of reverence for the word of God, brought about largely by the so-called 'Higher critics' of the last thirty years, the men who broke Spurgeon's heart, the Issachars of the nineteenth and early twentieth century, those 'knowing ones' who, like Issachar, thought that they knew better than God."

The two men walked on together in deep talk. Ralph learned that his companion was Robert J. Baring, principal of the great shipping firm, and of merchants and importers.

Baring was an educated man, and of considerable culture, and Ralph and he found that they had very much in common. But that which perhaps constituted the closest tie between them was the fact that both had lost their nearest and dearest, and were *left* to face the coming horrors of the Anti-christ reign, and the hideousness of the great Tribulation.

"God grant," Ralph said once, as they talked, "that when the moment comes, as come it will, that we are called upon to stand for God, or die for Him, that we may witness a good confession."

CHAPTER IV.

FORESHADOWINGS.

A MONTH had elapsed since the translation of the church. A new order in everything had arisen—Religious, Governmental, Social. The spirit of lawlessness grew fiercer and fouler each day, it is true, yet there *was* a supreme authority, a governmental restriction, that prevented the fouler, the more destructive passions of the baser kind of men and women, having full scope.

A curious kind of religion had been set up in many of the churches. The services were sensuous to a degree, and were a strange mixture of Romanism, Spiritism (demonology,) Theosophy, Materialism, and other kindred cults. Almost every week some new ode or hymn was produced, every sentiment of which was an applauding of man, for God was utterly ignored, and the key-note of the Harvard college "class Poem," for the year 1908, became the key-note of the Sunday Song of the "worshippers" in the churches:

> "*No* God for a gift God gave us—
> MANKIND ALONE must save us."

It was a curious situation, since it was "man" worshipping himself. Presently, the centre of worship would shift from man, to *The* Man of Sin—the Antichrist.

These religious services were held, as a rule, from twelve-thirty to one-fifteen on the Sunday once a day only, (without any *week*-night meetings.) They were held at an hour when, in the old-days, the congregations would have been home, or going home, from their services. But this arranged lateness was due to the fact, that there had grown up in all sections of society an ever-increasing lateness of retiring at night, coupled with a growth of indolence caused by every kind of sensual indulgence, not the least of which was gluttony. Music of a sensuous, voluptuous character formed a chief part of the brief Sunday services, and every item was loudly applauded as though the whole affair had been a performance rather than a professedly religious service.

Most of the interior arrangements in many of the old places of worship had been altered. The theatre style of thing—plush-covered tip seats, etc.—had taken the place of the old pews and the wooden seats. In many of these Sunday services, too, people of both sexes smoked at will—for smoking among women had become almost universal.

There were no Bibles, or Hymn books, the odes, etc., were printed on double sheets, after the fashion of theatre programmes, and, like them, contained numerous advertisements of the Sunday matinees and evening performances at the theatres, music-halls, etc.

All this had been brought about much more easily than would at first appear, until we remember one or two factors that had long been working silently, subtly among the attendants—mere church professors—of the various places of worship, such as, the insistance on shorter services, and fewer—for long, before the Rapture, the unspiritual had clamoured for a *single* service of the week, that of a late Sunday morning one. Then for years religious services (those of the Sunday) had grown more and more sensuous, unspiritual. Every real *spiritual* doctrine had first been denied, then expunged from the *essay* that had largely taken the place of the old-time sermon. Again, all spiritual restraints had now been taken away—the true believers, the Holy Spirit, every spiritually-minded, born-again pastor and clergyman.

The new Religion (it could not be called a Faith) was a universal one. The powers of the Priest-craft had invented a religion of the Flesh, fleshy to a degree. Every type of indulgence was permissible, so that men everywhere gloried in their religion, "having a form—but denying God."

The performances at all theatres, music-halls, etc., had grown rapidly worse and worse, in character,—licentiousness, animalism, voluptuousness, debauchery, these were the main features of the newer type of performances. Salome dances, and even the wildest, obscenest type of the *"can-can"* of the French, in its most promiscuous lascivious forms, were common fare on the varied English stages.

But if the stage was filthy and indecent, what could be said of the books! There was not a foulness or obscenity and indecency that was not openly, shamelessly treated in the bluntest of phraseology. Thousands of penny, two-penny, and three-penny editions of utter obscenity were issued daily. And the vitiated taste of the great mass of the people grew voraciously by feeding upon them.

Marriage was a thing of the dead past. There had been a growth of foul, subtle, hideous teaching *before* the translation of the church. Marriage had been taught (in many circles) to be "an unnecessary restraint upon human liberty." "Women"—it had been written, *absolved from shame,* shall be *owners* of themselves." "We believe" (the same writer had written) "in the sacredness of the family and the home, the legitimacy of *every* child, and the inalienable right of every woman to the absolute possession of herself."

All this foul seed-teaching of the days *before* the Translation of the Church, burst into open blossom and fullest fruit when once the restraint of *Christian* public opinion had been withdrawn from the earth.

The friendship between Ralph Bastin and Baring had grown with the days, and as they watched the rapid march of events, all heading towards ultimate evil, they talked of the possible *finale,* while they encouraged themselves in their God.

One evening, when they met, Baring said:

"I suppose there will soon come the time when no one will be able to trade without bearing "the mark of the Beast."

"Some new indication that way?" asked Ralph.

"I think so," Baring returned. "You remember that I told you that previous to the taking away of the Church, the vessels of my firm had been *tentatively* chartered for the transport of the various parts of the Temple to Jerusalem. To-day, the negotiations have been quashed by those who had previously approached us."

"For what reason?" asked Ralph.

"They gave no reason," Baring went on, "but I have not the slightest doubt, myself, that the real reason is this, that I have, of late, continually spoken warningly against Anti-christ."

"But how could that be known in circles purely Anti-christ?" Ralph's tones were eager; his eyes, too, were filled with a puzzled expression.

"You know," Baring returned, "what we were speaking of the other night, that now that the devil and his angels had been cast down from the air, they are (though invisible) yet actively engaged all about us on the earth?"

Ralph nodded assent.

"I believe, I am sure they are everywhere present." Baring smiled a little sadly, as he added, his eyes sweeping the room in a swift, comprehensive way: "There may be, there probably is, one or more present in this room, at this moment, their object espionage. They have doubtless been present when I have spoken against Anti-christ, and——"

"Yes, but this shipping matter of which you spoke, Bob, is a *Jewish* affair," interrupted Bastin, adding:

"For I presume, since the cargoes would be composed of the Temple parts, that it would be financed by Jewish capitalists, religionists, or what not? How then would Anti-christ have anything to do with it?"

Slowly, deliberately, almost solemnly Baring replied: "Lucien Apleon is a Jew!"

Bastin started sharply. Some idea of what his friend meant flashed upon him.

"Lucien Apleon!" he cried hoarsely. "But what——"

Baring broke in with: "I believe that Lucien Apleon will presently be *revealed* as the Anti-christ, and——"

The conversation had been going on in Ralph's Editorial office. It was now interrupted by a startling call over the tape-wire, and Baring suddenly realizing the hour, took a hurried temporary farewell of his friend.

An hour later Ralph was seated at his table penning

the "Prophet's chair" column for the next morning's issue of his paper. It was only natural, under the new order of life and thought that prevailed, that a daily paper, conducted on the lines of the 'Courier," should drop heavily in circulation. The "Courier" had so dropped, though it still paid to issue it.

"*My* enemies, the enemies of God and of righteousness," he murmured, as he took up his "Fountain," (he preferred a pen to a type-writer) "are, I am inclined to believe, the chief purchasers of the paper now, and they only buy it to see what I say from the 'Prophet's Chair.'"

For a moment, as was now his invariable custom, before beginning his daily message, he bowed his head and prayed for wisdom to write God's mind.

When next he lifted his head, and put pen to paper, he wrote with great rapidity, and without an instant's hesitation:

"Resuming the subject of which we wrote yesterday, we tried to show from Revelation XII, that the teaching was this, that, full of rage because of his casting out from the heavens, Satan, the great Dragon, the old Serpent, determined to destroy all lovers of God, that were yet found among mortals. But even Satan himself is a spirit, and 'cannot operate in the affairs of the world except through the minds, passions and activities of men.' He needs to embody himself in earthly agents, and to put himself forth in earthly organisms, in order to accomplish his murderous will.

"Through this wonderful Revelation of God to John, God makes known to us what that organism is, and how the agency and the domination of the enraged Dragon will be exerted in acting out his blasphemies, deceits,

and bloody spite. The subject is not a pleasant one,
but it is an important one. It also has features so startling and extraordinary that many may think it but a wild
and foolish dream. Nevertheless it is imperative that we
should all look at it, and understand it. God has evidently set it out for us to learn and know just how things
will eventually turn out.*

"John, 'in the Spirit,' finds himself stationed on the
sands of the sea—the same great sea upon which Daniel
beheld the winds striving in their fury. He beholds a
monstrous Beast rising out of the troubled elements. He
sees horns emerging, and the number of them is ten,
and on each horn a diadem. He sees the heads which
bear the horns, and these heads are seven, and on the
heads are names of blasphemy. Presently the whole
figure of the monster is before him. Its appearance is
like a leopard or panther, but its feet are the feet of a
bear, and its mouth as the mouth of a lion. He saw also
that the Beast had a throne, and power, and great authority. One of his heads showed marks of having been
fatally wounded and slain, but the death-stroke was
healed.

"He saw also the whole earth wondering after the
Beast, amazed at his majesty and power, exclaiming at
the impossibility of withstanding it, and celebrating its
superiority to everything. He beheld, and the Beast was
speaking great and blasphemous things against God,
blaspheming His name, His tabernacle, even them that
tabernacle in the Heaven the translated saints), assailing
and overcoming the saints on the earth, and wielding
authority over every tribe, and people, and tongue and

*The Apocalypse, by Joseph A. Seiss, D.D. p. p. 401.

nation. He saw also that all the dwellers on earth, whose names are not written in the book of life of the Lamb slain, did worship this Beast. And for forty-two months the monster holds its place and enacts its resistless will.

"This is the picture! What are we to make of it? What does it mean? How are we to understand it? It would seem to be a symbolic presentation of the political sovereignty of *this world at the final crisis.*

"The Beast has horns, and horns represent power. On these horns are diadems, and diadems are the emblems of regal dominion. The Beast is said to possess power, a throne, and great authority. He makes war. He exercises dominion over all tribes, and peoples, and tongues, and nations He is a monstrous Beast, including in his composition the four beasts of Daniel.

"From the interpreting angel we know that Daniel's four beasts denoted 'four kingdoms' that arose upon the earth. The identification thus becomes complete and unmistakable, that this monstrous Beast is meant to set before us an image of earthly sovereignty and dominion. And if any further evidence of this is demanded, it may be abundantly found in Rev. XVII. 9-17, where the same Beast is further described, and the ten horns are interpreted to be 'ten kings.'

"This Beast is therefore the embodiment of this world's political sovereignty in its last phase, in the last years of its existence. Daniel's beasts were successive empires, the Babylonian, the Medo-Persian, the Graeco-Macedonian, and the Roman. But the lion, the bear, the leopard, and the nameless ten-horned monster, each distinct in Daniel, are all united in one in Revelation.

"This Beast appears to be, undoubtedly, an *individual administration, embodied in one particular man.* Though upheld by ten kings or governments, they unite in making the Beast the one sole Arch Regent of their time.

"This he—the Beast, the Anti-christ—gets a grip of the nations, who willingly submit to his rule, being under the spirit of delusion, 'believing *the* lie' of the Anti-christ.

"Already, we see that this confederacy of nations is being called into an almost sudden existence. The seers of our nation, before this strange order of things that has arisen in our midst, since the taking away of the church, were wont to say to certain political changes—'at the back of all the known forces that have helped to bring so-and-so to pass, there almost *seems* to have been some unseen, unknown Master-mind at work.'

" 'Tis so now, and the startling events that are following each other so rapidly, are the product of a master-mind, the 'Man of Sin,' Anti-christ, the Beast who has been energized by Satan, the Old Dragon, who though he has not *yet* avowed himself, may be expected to do so any day or hour now.

"It will hardly be news to any one who reads this column regularly, that the building of the Temple which is to be reared in Jerusalem, by the Jews, who have largely returned to the 'Promised land' in unbelief, is being pushed on with the utmost celerity. The fact that, for some years previous to the Translation of the Church, all its parts, made to perfect scale, were prepared and fitted, enables the builders to erect this wonderful structure with almost magical speed.

"Simultaneous with this work, there has just appeared in Jerusalem, two remarkable men, who would appear to be Enoch and Elijah of old. These men are witnesses for God, and are testifying against Anti-christ.

"We say that these men would *appear* to be Enoch and Elijah, and not Moses and Elijah, as some, in the old days before the Rapture, had supposed. The allusion to water turned to blood, in the eleventh chapter of Revelation (which treats of God's two witnesses) very probably led some writers to connect the *first* of the two witnesses with Moses—since Moses turned water into blood.

"The main point of identification, we think, in the case of these two witnesses, however, lies in the fact that since it is appointed unto men *once* to die, the two witnesses must needs be men who have never passed through *mortal* death. *Moses did die,* hence it seems to us that he was disqualified from being one of the two witnesses, both of whom have presently to pass through mortal death in the streets of Jerusalem. Now Enoch and Elijah did *not* pass through mortal death, hence we believe the event will prove that these two witnesses are Enoch and Elijah.

"Each day that we pen this particular column we are conscious that it may be the last we shall pen, hence our anxiety to warn all our readers against the Anti-christ, and his lie—the strong delusion of 2 Thessalonians II 12."

For a few moments longer Ralph wrote on in this strain, then, just as he had completed the last sentence, his special Tape-wire rang him up. He summoned Charley to carry his *M.S.* sheets to the comp. room With a word to his Secretary, (who was divided from him by one thickness of wall only, communication being by a 'phone,) he turned to his Tape.

CHAPTER V.

CRUEL AS THE GRAVE!

L UCIEN Apleon's eyes held the cold, cruel malignity of a snake. His brows were cold, straight, unruffled. His smile held the polished brutality of the most Mephistophelian Mephistopheles.

Judith Apleon knelt at his feet, her beautiful face working painfully. A smile as cruel as his mouth crept into his eyes as he noted her grovelling, as he watched the anguish in her face.

She shuddered as she saw that smile creep into his eyes. She had seen it before—more than once. The first time had been among the glorious mountains of her beautiful Hungarian home. An old peasant woman, with the reputation of a witch, had scowled upon him, and had uttered a curse on him. The spot where the three had met was in a lonely pass. At the utterance of the curse he had cut the poor old hag down, with one fierce slash of his heavy riding whip. She had howled for mercy, and for reply he flogged the poor frail old prostrate form until life had fled, then, with a lifting spurn of his foot, he had hurled the body over the edge of that mountain pass, into the unknown depths of the ravine beyond. And all the time his eyes had smiled, as they smiled now—and Judith shuddered, for the smile was as cruel as the grave, and was a reflection of Hell.

She knew the diabolical cruelty which lay hidden behind that smile, and remembering the fate of those upon whom he had bent that smile, she sickened with a shuddering fear of her own life.

They had quarreled, that is to say she had *tried* to thwart him in a trifling thing. She hardly, herself, realized *what h*e was, or the power he possessed.

"Lucien," and her voice shook with the agony which filled her, with the fear that had her in its shuddering grip. "Lucien, don't look like that at me."

With an affrighted scream she cried: "Don't! Don't! Lucien! No one on whom I ever saw you look, as you look now, ever lived an hour, and——."

His gaze of diabolical hate hypnotized her. She wanted to take her eyes from his, but could not.

He made her no audible reply. He only smiled on. A faint cry, like the low scream of a terrified coney, escaped her. Her face paled until it was like the grey —white of a corpse.

"Spare me, Lucien, spare me——."

She would have said more, but the chill of his hellish smile froze the words upon her lips.

He never once changed his attitude. His left elbow rested on the corner of the mantel, the fingers of his right hand played with the gold watch-guard he wore.

A full minute elapsed, then with a cry of passionate, painful entreaty, she lifted her beautiful clasped hands, and wringing them in agony, cried:

"Lucien—Lucien—." Then a sob choked her.

For another long minute there was a tomb-like silence. He never moved a muscle of his face. The chill of the smile in his eyes deepened, and seemed, as it was bent upon her, to numb her faculties.

Her whole frame seemed to wilt under the ice of his smile. She shivered with the concentrated hate his eyes expressed.

Lower and lower she crouched at his feet. And as he saw her wilt and shiver the smile of Hell deepened in his cruel eyes.

Suddenly he spoke. The words were uttered in dulcet tones. But their meaning had, to her, the sentence of death, as softly, calmly, there fell from his lips:

"I have no further need of you! You are in my way!"

For one instant her eyes remained fixed upon his face. Then slowly her limbs relaxed, her body swayed lightly forward, and sank rather than fell upon the thick pile of the carpet.

With a low, mocking laugh Lucien Apleon turned away from the dead form. But before he passed out of the room he did a curious thing. A Bible rested on one of the shelves of the room, he took the volume from its place, opened it at the 13th of Revelation and taking a pen, he dipped it into the red ink, and ran a red line around the 15th verse of the chapter.

A moment later he had passed from the room.

The verse he had red-scored, read: "He had power to give life unto the *image* of the Beast, that the image of the Beast should both speak, and cause that as many as would not worship the image of the beast should be killed."

No wonder that Lucien Apleon smiled. For if presently, he was going to cause the *image* of the Beast to cause death to those who defied him, how much more could he himself strike dead by the power of the Satanic energy given to him.

Judith Apleon's body was conveyed to the crematorium and consumed. A doctor had certified heart-disease; there was no inquest. Lucien did not attend the funeral. The whole affair was carried through by the undertaker. There were no mourners.

The Anti-christ spirit is marked by "Without natural affection," one could not therefore expect Anti-christ himself to possess *any* affection.

CHAPTER VI.

"A REED LIKE A ROD."

E VENTS moved with startling rapidity. Events which, in the swift-moving times of the last years of the nineteenth century, would have occupied a decade to bring to pass, now occupied no more than the same number of days. The revived Roman Empire was an established fact. Moved by Satan, the ten kings had united to make Lucien Apleon their Emperor. The nations, having cast off all belief in the orthodoxy of the previous centuries, refusing to believe God's truth, utterly scouting it, in fact, they had laid themselves open to receive Anti-christ's lie, and had swallowed it wholesale.

Babylon had been rebuilt, and had become the *Commercial* centre of the reign of Lucien Apleon, even as Jerusalem was now to become his religious centre.

Ralph Bastin was still Editor of the "Courier," though each week, each day, in fact, he wondered if it would be his last of office, even as he often wondered if he might not have to seal his testimony as a God-inspired editor, with his blood, his life.

Already, all who, like himself, would live Godly, had to suffer bitter persecution. Many of the Godly had been found mysteriously murdered, and always the murders had been passed over by those who were in authority.

Ralph was on the point of leaving his office for lunch-

eon, (he always lunched in the city,) when a visitor
was announced.

"Rabbi Cohen, to see you, sir," announced Charley.

"Show him in at once," replied Ralph, and rising to
his feet he went to the door to meet his friend.

The Rabbi entered with a little eager run, and the
two men grasped hands heartily, their respective faces
glowing with the gladness they each felt.

As it had been with Tom Hammond and that other
Cohen, the Jew, who had shared in the translation of
the Church, so with the Rabbi who was now visiting
Ralph, he had been drawn to call upon Ralph, in the
first place, because of his editorial espousal of the Jewish
people and their interests.

Between Ralph and the Rabbi, there had grown up
a very strong friendship, and though for some weeks,
they had not met, each knew that the other's friendship
was as ever.

After a few ordinary exchanges between the pair, the
Rabbi, suddenly looked up eagerly, saying:

"I have come to say good-bye, to you, my friend,
unless, by any fortunate chance, I can persuade you to
accompany me, or, at least, follow me soon."

"Good-bye, Cohen?" cried Ralph, "Why—what—
where are you going?"

"To Jerusalem, Bastin!" There was a curious ring
of mixed pride and gladness in the manner of his saying
"Jerusalem."

"You know," he went on, "that we Cohens are the
descendents of Aaron, that we are of the priestly line.
I am the head of our family, and my people have chosen
me as the *first* High priest for our new Temple worship."

Brimming with his subject, he spoke rapidly, enthusiastically: "The Temple is to be formally opened on the tenth of September. The tradition among my people, and handed down to us in many of our writings is this, that the Great Temple of Solomon—opened in the seventh month, as all our scriptures, yours as well as ours, say—was dedicated and opened on a day corresponding with the modern tenth of September. Our new Temple will be opened on the tenth of this month."

On entering the room he had laid a long, cylinder-shaped japanned roll upon the table. This he now took up, took off the lid, and drew out a roll of vellum. Unrolling the vellum, he held the wide sheet out between his two outstretched hands, saying:

"I brought this on purpose for you to see, friend Bastin."

He smiled pleasantly as he added: "I expect you are the only Gentile who has seen this finished drawing."

For a few moments both men were silent. Ralph was speechless from amazement, the Rabbi from eager interest in watching his friend's amaze.

The "drawing," as the Rabbi had called it, was in reality a superb painting of the most marvelous structure possible to conceeive. The bulk of the vellum surface was occupied with an enormous oblong enclosure. The outer sides of the enclosure showing a most exquisite marble terracing, the capping of the marble wall was of a wondrous red-and-orange-veined dark green stone. The bronze gates were capped and adorned with massive inlayings of gold and silver, while the floral parts showed the colours of the precious stones used to produce each separate coloured flower.

A huge altar, the ascent to which, on three of the sides was by flights of wide steps, occupied the fore-

part of the courtyard inside the gates of the main
entrance—there were five entrances, each with its own
gates. Two entrances on each side of the oblong enclosure, and one at the courtyard end.

Beyond the altar was a huge brazen sea, resting upon
the hind-quarters of twelve bronze oxen. Beyond the
brazen sea was the temple itself, entered by a wide porch
of wondrous marble, the pillars of which were crowned
with golden capitals of marvellous workmanship. The
porch was surmounted by a dome. Then came the
temple proper, its form a square above a square, the
upper square surmounted by a huge dome, supported
upon columns similar to those found in the porch, and
in the base-square.

What the actual building must be like Ralph could
not conceive! The picture of it was a bewildering vision
of almost inconceivable loveliness.

Now and again he asked a question, the Rabbi, at his
side, delighted with his admiration, answering everything fully.

"What has your wonderful temple cost?" Ralph presently asked, as the picture was being rolled up, and
replaced in the japanned cylinder.

"Twenty million pounds, a full third of which has
been spent upon precious stones for studding the walls,
and gates, and pillars!"

Ralph gasped in amaze. "Twenty—million—pounds!"
He repeated the words much after the manner of a man
who, recovering from a swoon, says, "Where—am—I?"

They talked together for a few moments of the *how*
of the financing of such a costly undertaking. Then suddenly, Bastin faced his friend, a rare wistfulness in his
face and in his voice, as he said:

"I wish, dear Cohen, you, and your dear people could see how futile all this work is! I do not want to hurt you by speaking of Jesus of Nazareth. But suffer me to say this, that probably the only references which God's word makes to this Temple of yours, are in Daniel xii. 11 and in the Christian New Testament, Matthew xxiv. Mark xiii 2, 2 Thessalonians ii 14, and Revelation xi 1, *and there it is mentioned in connection with Judgment.* In the first verse of *our* eleventh of Revelation, the temple is to be measured, but it is with a reed *like a rod.* Not the ordinary measuring reed, but like a *rod,* the symbol of Judgment.

"And that, dear Cohen, will be the end of your beautiful temple—it will be destroyed in Judgment, and soon—all too soon—it will be cursed and defiled by the abomination of desolation of which your beloved prophet Daniel speaks, in the twelfth chapter and the eleventh verse."

With a sudden new eagerness, but as sad as he was eager, he said: "In your extremity, and in your desire to be established in the land of your fathers, you talk of making a seven years covenant with Lucien Apleon, Emperor of the European confederacy?"

Cohen, evidently impressed by Ralph's manner, nodded an assent, but did not speak.

"Oh, Cohen, my friend, my friend!" Ralph went on. "Would to God you and your people had your eyes open to the true character of that man, Lucien Apleon! If you had, you would see from your own prophets that he was prophesied to be your foe. Remember Daniel nine, twenty-seven (according to the modern chaptering and verses) "He shall confirm the covenant with many for *one week*: (a week of years, of seven years) and in the midst of the week (at the end of the first three and a half years) he shall cause the sacrifice and the oblation to cease, and on the battlements shall be the idols of the desolator."

Cohen's face was a picture of wondering amaze. Twice his lips parted as though he would speak, but no sound came from them, and Ralph went on:

"I could weep with very anguish of soul, dear friend, at all that you, and every truly pious Jew will suffer; when, at the end of the three years and a half ('the midst of the week') the foul fiend whom you are all trusting so implicitly, will suddenly abolish your daily sacrifice of the morning and evening lamb, and will set up an image of himself, which you, and all the *Godly* of your race, will refuse to worship. Then will begin your awful tribulation, 'the time of Jacob's deadly sorrow.'

"It is in your own Scriptures, dear friend, if you would but see it. And in *our* New Testament, in Matthew twenty-four, which is *all Jewish* in its teaching, our Lord and Saviour, foretold all this as to come upon your people. He even showed them to be in their own land, saying, 'let them which are in Judea flee into the mountains . . . . and pray that your flight be not on the Sabbath day:' (for you Godly Jews would not go beyond Moses' 'Sabbath day's journey,' and Anti-christ's myrmidons would then soon overtake you.)"

As if to jerk the talk into a new channel. Cohen said, almost abruptly:

"Why do you say, my friend, that *our* temple, tne temple which we shall dedicate on the tenth of this month, has probably so few mentions in the Scriptures, and those in judgment. When *we* say that the whole of the nine last chapters of our prophet Ezekiel are taken up with it. Nearly all our plans have followed the directions, the picture of Ezekiel's Temple?"

"That temple, sketched in Ezekiel," replied Ralph, "is the millennial temple. There was no temple in the nineteen hundred odd years between the destruction of Jerusalem and its temple, and the translation of 'The church,' a few months ago. There could be no temple as regards God's people—The Church—because all that nineteen hundred years was a *spiritual* dispensation. God's Temple then was composed of living stones, wherein a *spiritual* priesthood offered up spiritual sacrifices.

"But to go back to the temple described by Ezekiel in the last nine chapters of his prophecy—this is the temple which will be reared in the Millennium, but it will *not be* in Jerusalem. Read carefully over all that Ezekiel's description, and you will see that when your Messiah, our Christ, comes to reign for that wonderful time of a thousand years of perfect righteousness, that your land—the land given in promise by God to your father Abraham—is to be *re*-divided (Ezekiel forty-five one to five). Ezekiel's Temple, and the division of the land, stand and fall together, and it is a subject that cannot be symbolized.

"Now when the land is divided into straight lines, 'a holy oblation' is commanded of sixty square miles—if the measurement be by *reeds,* or fifteen square miles if the measurement be by *cubits*. This oblation land will be divided into three parts. The northern portion will be for the priests, and the new temple will be in the midst. The second division of land, going South will be for the Levites. And the third, the most Southerly portion, will contain Jerusalem. So that that temple of the

Millenium—Ezekiel's temple—will be fully thirty miles from Jerusalem.

"Solomon's temple, and the one your people have just reared are both situated on Mount Moriah, but Ezekiel's temple will not be on Mount Moriah, for according to Isaiah two, two, 'It shall come to pass in the last days, that the mountain of Jehovah's House shall be established in the top of the mountains, and shall be exalted above the hills; and all nations shall flow unto it.'

"Read carefully, dear Cohen, your own loved Scriptures (in this connection, especially Isaiah 50) and you will see that Gentiles shall help, financially, as well as by manual labor to build the place, which shall make the place of Jehovah's feet glorious—that must be His *Temple,* and *not the city.* Though Gentiles will also help to build the walls of your new city of Jerusalem in *that* day."

For fully another half hour the subject was pursued. Cohen was amazed, puzzled, but because his mind was not an open one to receive the Truth—nothing blinds and obstructs like a preconceived idea—he failed to grasp the Scriptural facts as presented by Ralph.

The moment came for the farewell word between them. "I may never see you again on earth, dear friend," Ralph remarked. "For, believe me, the day is near at hand when all of us who will cleave to *our* God, *your* God —the God of Abraham, Isaac and Jacob, will have to seal our testimony with our blood.

"In three years and a half you, dear Cohen, and all the Godly ones of your race, will be at issue with Lucien Apleon, for according to your own prophet, Daniel (apart from our *New* Testament Scriptures) he, the 'Anti-christ, will autocratically put a stop to your sac-

rifices in your Temple, and will set up his own image
to be worshipped, and if you will not worship that image,
or if you do not succeed in fleeing to a place of safety,
your lives will be forfeited. May God bless you dear,
dear friend, and lead you into the Truth of His own
plain statements of the facts you have to face."

Cohen was quiet, subdued, almost sad. Then, as if to
bridge an awkward moment, he said, with a forced
eagerness:

"Why not come to the opening of the Temple yourself, instead of sending a representative to report to your
paper?"

Ralph shook his head; "I could not get away, dear
friend."

He did not voice the actual thing which weighed with
him, that any day now h᷉ might cease to be Editor of the
"Courier."

The two men shook hands, and parted as men part
who never expect to meet again.

Bastin left alone dropped into a "brown study." He
was suddenly recalled to the present, by the arrival of
the mail. The most important packet bore the handwrit-
ing of Sir Archibald Corlyon Ralph's proprietor.

He smiled as he broke the envelope, recalling the
thought of his heart only twenty minutes ago, and wondering whether his foreboding was now to be verified.

The letter was as kindly in its tone as Sir Archibald's
letters ever were. But it was none the less emphatic.
After kindliest greetings, and a few personal items, it
went on:

"All the strange happenings of the past months have
strangely unnerved me. I cannot understand things, 'I
dunno where I are,' as that curious catch-saying of the

nineteenth century put it. I live like a man in a troubled dream, a night-mare. Several members of our
church have been taken, and I, who prided myself on my
strict churchmanship, have been left behind. My boon
companion, the rector of our parish, a man who always
seemed to me to be the beau ideal clergyman, he too is
left, and is as puzzled and angry as I am. I think he is
more angry and mortified than I am, because his pride
is hurt at every point, since, as the Spiritual head (nominally at least) of this parish, he has not only been passed
over by this wonderful translation of spiritual persons,
but being left behind he has no excuse to offer for it.

"The curate of our church and his wife, whom we
always spoke of as being 'a bit *peculiar*,' they disappeared
when the others did. By the bye, Bastin, good fellow,
what constitutes '*peculiarity*,' in this sense? It seems to
me now, that to be out and out for God—as that good
fellow and his wife were, as well as one or two others
in our parish—is the real peculiarity of such people. God
help us, what fools we have been!

"Our village shopkeeper, a dissenter, and a much-
vaunted *local* preacher, is also left behind, but his wife
was taken. A farmer, a member of our own church,
who used to invite preachers down from the Evangeliza-
tion Society, London, is gone, but his wife, a strict
churchwoman like myself—but a rare shrew—is left.

"But to come to the chief object of my letter, I am
afraid you will be sorry—though perhaps not altogether
unprepared for what I have to say—'*I have sold the
'Courier*.' It may be the only daily paper, (as you wrote
me the other day) that 'witnesses for righteousness,'
but my mind is too harrassed by all this mysterious
business of the *Translation* of men and women, to think

of anything else but the future, and what it will bring. I have sold the paper to Lucien Apleon (through one of his agents, of course, since now that he is made Emperor of this strangely constituted confederation of kings and countries) he cannot be expected to personally transact so small a piece of business as the purchase of a daily paper."

Ralph lowered the letter-sheet, a moment, and a weary little smile crept into his face.

"I might have guessed that Apleon would have done this," he mused, "if he is, as I believe, the Anti-christ!"

He lifted the letter again, and read on:

"He wanted to take possession at once, and give me £5,000 extra as a retiring fee for you. But I was obstinate on this point, and told his agent that he could not have possession until a month from today.

"Between this and then I shall hope to see you, dear Bastin. I want to see you very much on my own account. Your utterances from 'The Prophet's chair,' have aroused strange new thoughts and desires within me, and I want you to help me to a clearer view of the events of the near future. Then, as to the sundering of our business relations, you know me so well that you know I shall treat you handsomely when you retire from the Editorship.

"'Talking of finance, what special use can money be to a man like me now, if all that you have lately written in the 'Courier'—as to *the future*—be true?"

The letter wound up most cordially. Then there followed a "P. S."

"My old friend, the Rector of the parish, who has always been keen on theatricals—he would have made a better actor than parson—is having the church seated with plush-covered tip-seats like a theatre, and proposes to have a performance every Sunday Evening, and as often in the week as funds, and interest in the affair, will warrant. Good Heavens! What has the world come to? Then only to think that England's King, is under the supreme rule of a Jew, whose antecedents no one appears to know—that is to say, previous to his meteoric-like appearance when he was twenty-five. 'How are the mighty fallen!"

"How, indeed!" murmured Ralph, with a sigh, as he let the letter fall on his table.

For a moment or two he stared straight in front of him, then, half aloud, he murmured:

"A month only! God help me to make good use of the thirty days! If I can but wake up some of the people of this land to the real position of affairs, I shall be only too thankful."

For a few moment's longer he sat on, deep in thought. Then suddenly he started sharply, grew alert in every sense, and sounded a summons for his messenger boy. When the lad appeared, he asked:

"Do you know if Mr. Bullen is on the premises?"

"Yus, sur, he is!"

"Ask him to step this way, at once, please!"

George Bullen, was a keen, up-to-date young journalist, a man of thirty-two only, but with a fine record as regarded his profession. A close personal friendship existed between his chief and himself, for he had been wholly won to God through Ralph's efforts.

In a few words Ralph explained to the younger man, the changes that were near at hand. Then continuing:

"But while you and I, George, represent 'The Courier,' we will make it all the power for God and for humanity that lies in our power. Though I am not sure that we can do much with *humanity,* now. The strong delusion has got such an almost universal grip upon the race, that they will gladly, eagerly swallow all the lie of the Arch-liar, the Anti-christ. In the old days, before the translation of the church, the Bible spoke of 'the whole world lieth in the arms of the Wicked One,' and that is truer than ever now. Well, George, *we* must do all *we* can.

"But now to the chief thing for which I sent for you. The new temple at Jerusalem is to be opened on the tenth. I want you to go, to represent the 'Courier.' What I am especially anxious for you to do, is to note everything that will show the true *inwardness* of things, so that the little time left to us, on the dear old paper, shall be a time of holy witness for God.

"Your knowledge of the East, your acquaintance with Yiddish, and Syrian and Hebrew, the very swarthiness of your skin, and blackness of your hair, dear boy, may all serve you in good stead. For, if you feel led to it, I should suggest that you adopt that Syrian costume I once saw you in. This course would have many advantages, for while you could the more readily mix with the people, and obtain *entree* often where you otherwise could not, your identity as representative of 'The Courier,' would not be made known.

"I am not sure, George, but that if you presented yourself as our representative, that all kinds of obstacles might not be put in the way of your obtaining information, or, more likely, in transmitting it. You might even be quietly put out of the way. Spare no expense, dear boy, where other men spend five pounds, spend a hundred, if it will serve us better."

For a time the two men held deep consultation. Then

when they gripped hands in parting, each commended the other to God.

George Bullen started for the East next afternoon. His stock of Eastern garments was full and varied, and not one Eastern in a million would have known him from a Syrian native.

CHAPTER VII.

GEORGE BULLEN was no stranger to Jerusalem, yet it was a strange Jerusalem that met his sight as he entered it by the Jaffa gate. For interest, picturesqueness, even amusement, there is no time so rich as at early morning, at the Jaffa gate.

Bullen had been perfectly familiar, in the old days (eight years ago) with the scene, but there were differences this morning. The long strings of donkeys and camels, laden to within the proverbial "last straw," and led by foul-smelling, unkempt Bedouins were there, as usual, in spite of the fact that railways now ran in every direction. Eastern women, robed in their loose blue cotton wrapper garments—sleeping, as well as day attire —were there in galore, only now all of them walked unveiled, whereas, in the old days, most of them were veiled.

Pilgrims from every land were pouring into the city. The cafes were crowded. The aroma of strong black coffee was often *fortunately,* stronger than the less pleasant odours of the insanitary streets.

Early as it was, the money changers were doing a stirring trade. Water-carriers moved about with their monotonous cry of *"moyeh,"* supplemented, in some cases, by the same word in English—*"Water."*

Market garden produce, the finest in the world, and now proving how literally Palestine, under the fertilizing power of the *"latter* rain," had become "a fruitful

garden," was piled everywhere about at the sides of the
streets. Cauliflowers thirty-six inches around, with
every other vegetable equally fine, melons, lemons,
oranges, grapes, tomatoes, asparagus, onions, leeks, let-
tuce, water-cress, even garlic, all were here, with turbaned dealers sitting cross-legged among the produce.

Early as it was, crowds of American, English, and
Continental tourists were abroad, their gleaming white
drill attire and tobies and helmets, conspicuous among
the grander colour of the natives.

But George Bullen had seen all this many times before,
his eyes now took but little note of the streets and their
contents, except that he noted the fact under the
new order of things, since the Jews had come into
possession of the city, that there was scarce a Moslem
of any kind to be seen, and that most of the tumble-
down, smaller houses, of a few years back, had been
pulled down, and that the streets in consequence had
been considerably widened. Hundreds of new houses of
bungalow type, had taken the places of those pulled
down. Most of these were built on the "Frazzi" system,
or else after the fashion known as reinforced concrete.

All these changes were note-worthy, and full of meaning, but George Bullen's eyes and attention were almost
wholly absorbed by the Temple that crowned Mount
Moriah. He had not, of course, seen that wonderful
painting on Vellum which Rabbi Cohen had shown Ralph
Bastin. It is true he had seen photographs and sketches
reproduced in the English illustrated papers. But none
of these had prepared him for the actual.

Robed in his Syrian garb, and looking for all the
world like the "real article," he passed through the cos-
mopolitan crowd always making his way upwards to

where the marble and gold of the wonderful Temple reared itself.

Arrived outside the great main gates, he stood awed at the wonder and magnificence of all that he saw. The whole structure was complete. Not a pole or plank of scaffolding was left standing, no litter or rubbish heaps were to be seen; every approach, every yard of the enclosure was beautifully swept. A few officials, in a remarkable uniform moved here and there about the great enclosure.

For two hours George Bullen moved slowly round the Temple, making long pauses at intervals, and taking in every item of the wondrous architecture and still more wondrous ornamentation. When he finally left the Mount, and took his way down the wide, steep decline —the whole of this wide road was composed of marble blocks, reminding him of the Roman Appian way—his mind was in a whirl, his head ached with the glare of the sun on the gold, and with the deep concentration of his sight upon so much colour and glitter. Again and again he paused, and looked upwards and backwards, he had a difficulty in tearing himself away. But he had much to do, and could not afford to linger.

*   *   *   *   *

It was the day before the official opening of the Temple. Jerusalem was thronged—inside and outside, for Jerusalem, (according to Zechariah ii. 4) was "inhabited *as* a town *without walls*." The environs, and the suburbs had spread in every direction. For the first time in the history of the world, the hills, Gareb and Goath, *outside* Jerusalem, had, a few years before this, been covered with villas, bungalows, hotels, etc., absolutely fulfilling Jeremiah xxxi. 38-40.

Lucien Apleon's Palace, which had been built concurrently with the Temple, and which, in its way, was almost as gorgeous a building, was filled with the ten Kings of the Confederacy, and their suites.

Soldiers of every one of the ten nationalities—though all wearing one uniform, save that the "facings" were different to denote the land to which they belonged— were everywhere to be seen.

Itinerant venders moved about among the throngs bawling their chief ware—"Programs for the Temple, to-morrow." George Bullen bought one of the Programs.

It was an amazing production, and as blasphemous as it was amazing. It was most sumptuously got up, printed in a style unknown to the days of even the end of the first decade of the 20th century.

But before he began to read the order of the events, or even to note the marks of sumptuousness of the appearance of the program, his attention was arrested by a bold, curious hieroglyphic which headed the program. This figuring was in richest purple and gold, and bore this form:

For a long time he puzzled over the sign. Then, suddenly a memory returned to him. One night when Ralph

Bastin had been speaking to him about the Anti-christ he had said:

"Here is a curious thing, George! I have just read in the Revelation, thirteen, eighteen, that The Number of the Beast—the Anti-christ—is THE Number of MAN; and his number is 666." Now this number, *in the Greek,* is made up of two characters which stand for the name of Christ, with a third character, the figure of a crooked serpent put between them—the name of God's Christ, the Messiah, turned into a devil sacrament (i. e. oath of fidelity.)

"Ralph would have shown me the sign, I know," Bullen mused, "but that at the very moment we were talking together, there came that scare of fire in the stereo room, and we both rushed away. But now I know that this sign on the program is the 'Mark of the Beast,' and that it *signifies the oath of Fidelity to Anti-christ.*"

He caught his breath sharply, as he murmured:

"So it has begun! He has begun to show his hand!"

Then he let his eyes take in the contents of the program.

Beneath the Hieroglyphic was the greeting:

"To ALL THE WORLD!

APLEON, EMPEROR,

by the election of
MAN.

Commands the following events in connection
with the Dedication and
opening of the Temple at Jerusalem.

4-30 p. m. 9th Sept., year 1 of Apleon.
(Subject to minor alterations.)

Appointment of the High Priest elect,
by the Emperor.

Address by The High Priest.

Confirmation of the 7 years Covenant
betweeen the Hebrew Nation and the Emperor.

Affirmatory Signatures and Seals affixed.

Sign of the Sacrament
to be distributed and donned by all present.

6-30 p. m. Bureaus will be opened all over the city, and in the immediate neighbourhood of the Temple for the free distribution of the sacramental signs, with directions for wearing the same. The donning of the sign will be, of course, entirely voluntary.

"For how long," murmured Bullen to himself, "will this be voluntary?"

He continued his reading:

"At 7-30 a. m. 10th Sept. The Dedication of the Temple. The procession of Kings, headed by Apleon, Emperor of the World, will start from the Apleon Palace at 7-0 a. m. Imperial troops will line the way.

"Fanfare of trumpets will greet the procession on its arrival at the Temple Gates.

"Opening ode will be sung by 1,000, singers massed in the courtyard.

"Ceremony inside will commence by the investiture of the High Priest with his glorious robes of office, the investiture will be performed by the Emperor.

"The 7 years Covenant to be read aloud by the High Priest.

"Ode of Adoration of the Emperor to be sung by the Priests, choristers, and others.

"The ceremony is to be held at the above early hour, that there may be no undue exposure to the heat of the later fore-noon.

In pursuance with the liberty of these more enlightened days, all persons may worship with covered or uncovered heads, as may seem fit to each person. This applies to Jews and Jewesses also, and, (N. B.) there will be no division of sex for the Jew and Jewess, they will worship together. The days of the *grille* are past.

"LONG LIVE THE EMPEROR!"

———

"Of all the extraordinary productions—!" murmured George Bullen. He did not finish his sentence, he would have been puzzled to have found terms to have expressed all that he felt.

"I wonder if these programs can be procured in London?" he went on.

A seller passed him at that moment, and he bought a second program, to send to Ralph Bastin.

They had made an arrangement, before parting, that everything—letters, wireless, and all other messages—should be sent in code, and to an address, and under a name that should not be recognized as having any connection with the 'Courier'—"if," Ralph had added quietly, "there are no demons present here who can divulge our talk."

This was always one of the difficulties that the godly, at that time, had to contend with, the ignorance of how far *invisible* demons could spy upon, and report their sayings and doings.

Hour by hour, the streets grew denser, for each hour

brought new arrivals, and always some of the *elite* of the earth. To George Bullen, with the journalist instinct, there was "copy" everywhere, and he was not slow to take full notes.

Things were quieter from one to four, for the heat, in the open, was almost unbearable. At four o'clock, Bullen was close by the chief gate of the Temple. He would watch the arrival of the chief actors in the first part of the great ceremonies.

Through the mighty hosts of acclaiming peoples which lined that wide marble upward road, King after King rode, all on white horses. Merchant princes from Babylon; Royal princes from many lands.

The last of the Kings to arrive was the King of Syria. At the gate, close to where George Bullen was standing, the horse of the Syrian monarch grew restive.

Quick to seize an opportunity of getting into the Temple to see the ceremony, George caught the rein of the horse, and with a soothing word and touch, led the beast through the gate, flinging back a word in Syrian to the King in the saddle.

Hearing his own tongue, and noting the garb of his horse's leader, the King flung a word of thanks to George, who led the horse right up to the door of the sanctuary.

Each monarch kept his saddle. Five were drawn up on one side, and five on the other. They waited for Apleon. A moment or two only, then amid a thunder of acclaim of "Long live the World's Emperor!" Lucien Apleon, the Anti-christ, the Man of Sin, riding a jet black horse, cantered through the gate.

He was a marvellous figure of a man. In stature he was nearer seven feet than six. His form as erect as a

Venetian mast. His costume was strange, but very striking, and gave him a regality of appearance.

It was partly Oriental, partly occidental, and consisted of a curious-toned darkish green military tunic, heavily-frogged with gold, and with a wide, gold-braid collar. The buttons of the tunic were separate emeralds set in circles of diamonds, and enclosed in a wide circlet of gold. He wore white knee-breeches, and high Hessian boots, adorned at the heels with gold spurs. Over his shoulders, clasped at the neck with a large gold-and-precious-stone buckle of the same mysterious form as the hieroglyphic crest at the head of the Programs, he wore a wonderful burnouse of white and gold fleece, the gold predominating over the white, and flashing fiercely, gorgeously in the sun. His leonine head was surmounted with a dazzling covering that was neither a crown, a mitre, nor a turban, but partook of the nature of all three. It was profusely bedecked with the most costly of precious stones. The largest diamond ever seen, shaped as an eight-pointed star, and measuring nearly six inches from point to point, was set in the front-centre of the mitre-turban-crown. With the sun shining upon it, it was impossible to gaze upon the diamond.

Riding up to the door of the porch of the Temple, his horse's fore-hoofs resting on the upper of the four steps, he paused only to return the salutes of the ten kings, then flung himself from the saddle, and waited a moment until his horse was led away. Then turning outwards towards the way by which he had come, he surveyed the scene below him.

Never in the history of the world had anything more wonderful been seen. Several million people were gathered—streets were blocked; walls of the city, roofs of the houses and palaces and public buildings were packed. Every window that faced the mount was crowded. Flags flew everywhere within the city, and beyond the walls, where hundreds of thousands of acclaiming people were gathered, every eye was directed towards that Temple entrance where Anti-christ, the World's Emperor stood.

As he turned to face the millions of acclaiming people, a gun was fired from the grounds of his palace, and at the same instant, a ball of white, which had hung at the head of the flag-staff on the roof of his palace, suddenly broke, and there swept out upon the light breeze, an enormous white silk flag, the centre of which bore the mystic inscription that had already appeared on the official programs, and which he wore in gold jewels for a buckle of his bernouse.

The eyes of Apleon flashed with a curious pride as he saw the great white flag break in the air, while a smile, diabolical as Hell itself, curled his lips. It seemed almost as though it was to see that damnable challenge flung forth to the wind, that he had turned, more than to acknowledge the acclaim of the gathered millions of the deceived, lie-deluded people.

A moment later, he turned into the Temple. The ten kings, Babylonian merchant-princes, and others of note following.

George Bullen, walking directly behind the King of Syria, passed in with the others.

CHAPTER VIII.

THE INVESTITURE.

A GREAT hush fell upon those who gathered within that Temple. It was not an awe from the sense of the divine—for God was not there in His glory and power, since Anti-christ's spirit filled the place. It was not the awe of silence and subjection to the world's greatest ruler—though, presently, something of that would come upon those gathered when they had eyes, ears, and mind for Apleon the Emperor. Neither was the silence one of curiosity in the character of the service in which they had been called to take part. The hush upon the assembly was one of wonder and amaze at the splendour of the Temple's interior in which they found themselves.

Gold—there was no silver—, precious stones, sandal-wood, marbles such as had never been seen by any eye before, all fashioned into a wondrous style of architecture peculiarly unique, yet withal holding a perfect harmony—such is (not a description, for a description, in detail would baffle the clearest mind and cleverest pen) —a bold mention of a few of the chief materials.

The artist—architect—he must have been as much an artist as an architect to have designed the style—had taken *some* ideas from the description, in Ezekiel, of the Millennial Temple. There was the palm, the cherub with two faces, (the young lion and the man) "so that the face of a young lion was on the one side toward the palm, and the face of a man on the other side toward the palm."

The vine and the pomegranite were there. In spite of the most profuse detail all was rendered with a perfection of minuteness, while throughout the whole of the interior the harmony of colour was beyond praise—and beyond description.

For the technical skill exhibited in each separate item of colour, carving, and "cunning" workmanship, had, with truest artistic sense, been subordinated to that wondrous balance of the whole appearance that went to make up the amazing harmony that was as a veritable atmosphere in the place. To combine in a chromatic scheme so much brilliance and colour without even a suspicion of gaudiness, or the *bizarre,* was a triumph of art.

The light in the place was a true adjunct to the effects produced by the wondrous composition of the blended glory and colour. There was no window anywhere, but "Radiance," the newest light of the day, tempered by rose-pink and palest electric blue prisms, filled the place with a wondrous radiance, while at the same time the eye could not detect the various spots where the separate lights were located.

The company gathered was in harmony with the place, since the many otherwise gaudy tints of costume and uniform were softened, blended, and harmonized by the power of colour-tone of the prisms through which the otherwise fierce, flashing "Radiance" was shed.

The *outer* temple interior—the place where the brilliant throng was gathered—would hold a thousand persons comfortably. (There was no seat in Solomon's temple, as there was no seat in the Tabernacle, which was a symbol of the ever unfinished work of the earthly priesthood.) And there was no seat here, save a throne-chair of gold, ivory, mother-of-pearl, and precious stones, that occupied the centre of a magnificent dais just in front of the entrance into the very small "Holy of Holies." A wonderful curtain of purple velvet—not the fine twined linen as of old—screened off this narrow strip of the interior, from the larger outer section. The curtain was worked with marvellous needlework in gold and pearls of almost priceless value, the pattern being a wonderful blending of cherubim, palm, and pomegranate.

On entering the building The Emperor Apleon, seated himself on the Throne, when each person present made a deep bow of obeisance. One man only remained upright—George Bullen. Taking advantage of his position behind a marble pillar, he held himself erect. Had he been detected, he would have rapturously sacrificed his life rather than have bent to the Anti-christ.

The platform of the dais, on which the throne-chair stood, was reached by three wide marble steps that sprang from the floor-level. At the foot of these steps, Cohen the High-priest elect, stood clothed in a single garment of pure white linen, that reached from his shoulders to his feet. Attendant priests stood by, each holding one garment or ornament, as the case might be, ready for the investiture.

Apleon rose from his throne, a magnificent, but a sardonic figure for all that. As he rose, soft, weird music came from an angle where a screen of palm-ferns was placed. Though mechanical, the music was of an exquisite character.

Then suddenly, swelling above the low weird music, came the voices of a score or more white-robed priests chanting:

"Hear, O Israel, the Lord thy God is one God!"

George Bullen's eyes were fixed upon the face of Apleon, and he noted the mocking, contemptuous smile that curled his lips at the language of the chant.

As the chant finished, Cohen turned and faced Apleon, and slowly climbed the steps. The music had ceased now, and, amid an absolute silence, Apleon took "the embroidered coat" from the offered hands of one of the subordinate priests. The garment was of white linen wonderfully, beautifully embroidered. It reached from the shoulders to the feet and fitted the body closely, a draw-string of white linen tape fastening the sleeves at the wrists, and drawing the breast of the vestment close about.

A linen girdle "four fingers wide," and long enough when tied to reach the feet, was next put about Cohen by Apleon. Then a third priest handed the Emperor, "The Robe of the Ephod." This was a long, loose garment of Royal blue satin, with a wide neck-opening, the opening bound with a wide gold band. The Robe was slipped over the head, and it dropped to the feet of the High-priest. Upon the lower hem of the Robe was a rich, deep fringe of alternate blue, purple, and scarlet tassels made in the form of pomegranates. Between each pome-granate was a golden bell.

Still amid an absolute silence, the investiture pro-ceeded. Apleon took the costly and beautiful Ephod of a fourth priest. This vestment was in two pieces, one for the front, the other for the back. They were joined together, at the shoulders, by bands of wide gold braid, and buckled with two of the Anti-christ covenant badges. Apleon had provided himself with these, and no one probably, save George Bullen, noticed of what the bucklings consisted. But nothing escaped Bullen, for while the attention of everyone else in the place was given only in a *general* way to the robing of the High Priest, *his* whole and absolute attention was concentrated on Apleon, all that he did, every varying expression of his handsome but sardonic face, and every movement of his fingers.

Another priest handed "The curious girdle of the Ephod." But, unlike the ordained adjunct, as given in Exodus, in this case it was a separate piece, and instead of being of the same stuff, was a cunningly worked band of gold studded with many gems. The girdle handed to Apleon, fastened with a clasp. The clasp was worth a Jew's ransom, and like the breast-plate—presently to be slung about the neck of Cohen—was a gift to the Temple by Apleon.

But the gift was accursed, for among the curiously, twisted gold of the clasp, the "Mark of the Beast" could be traced, if carefully scrutinized.

The Ephod Girdle being clasped, a priest handed the breastplate to the Emperor. It should, according to the Mosaic command, have been made of the same material as the Ephod—"of gold, of blue, of purple, of scarlet, and of fine twisted linen."

But in this case it was made of gold, and slung by a gold chain about the High-priest's neck.

The gold filigree setting for the stones, held within its cunning workmanship that same damnable sign—"The Mark of the Beast," though only a very keen, clever eye would have detected the foul hieroglyphic among the twistings of gold patterning. The whole plate was about ten inches square, the centre divided by gold ribs, across and across, into twelve sections, each section holding a separate precious stone of fabulous wealth. Just for a moment **or** two the wondrous mechanical music stole out again upon the silence. Lovers of music recognized part of Schubert's "Unfinished Symphony." What wondrous melody there was in the fragment! The priests' voices chanted again, and all the time the face of Apleon wore its mocking smile. Reading from the top—right to left, as the breastplate hung on the breast—the stones **and their significance ran as follows:**

CARBUNCLE,	TOPAZ	SARDIUS
Zebulun.	*Issachar.*	*Judah.*
DIAMOND	SAPPHIRE,	EMERALD,
Gad.	*Simeon*	*Reuben.*
AMETHYST,	AGATE	LIGURE,
Benjamin.	*Manasseh*	*Ephraim.*
JASPER,	ONYX	BERYL,
Naphtali.	*Asher*	*Dan.*

The last piece of this wonderful Robing, was the Mitre. It was really a turban of pure white linen, an oblong shield-shaped plate of pure gold, being attached to the fullness of the deep, front roll of the turban. Engraved in Hebrew characters upon the plate, were the words: "HOLINESS TO THE LORD." Here again, keen and practised eyes would have detected the foul sign of the "man of sin," among the wondrous, and delicate chasing of the gold around the Hebrew lettering.

It has taken twenty times longer to record this robing than the time actually employed. As a matter of fact it occupied but a few minutes. Then, at last, the work was complete, and the silence was broken.

It was the Emperor who spoke: "Behold the Priest of the Most High God!" he cried.

Every soul present, save George Bullen, was more or less under the spell of the Arch-Deceiver, or they would have caught the sneer in the rich full voice, even as George Bullen caught it.

True to his journalistic instinct, as well as to his new desire as a Christian, to know well the Word of God, Bullen had read over, the night before, the passages in Exodus and Leviticus, relating to the robing of the High-priest, and had been struck with this fact, that the High-priest himself did *nothing,* took no *active* part in his robing. Moses, *as God's representative,* did *everything.*

Now as he recalled this, and while he considered why Apleon should have "acted valet" to a Jew priest, there recurred, with startling power to Bullen, the words of prophecy by Daniel, concerning the "Man of Sin:" "he shall exalt himself, and magnify himself above every God—"

"He has purposely chosen to do this robing business, quietly setting himself up as God," was the thought of Bullen. There was no time for further musing. The newly-invested High-priest was speaking:

"Bring hither the '*Torah*'—Roll of the Law."

A serious-faced young Jew, a praying shawl over his head, bore towards the High-Priest—the parchment scroll loosely-cased in a silken slip-off. As he bore the sacred roll he reverently kissed the tassels of the draw-string of the silken slip.

The attendant drew off the cover, and dropping it across his left shoulder, unrolled the scroll, and held it extended for the High-priest to read.

Cohen made a sign to a priest who held a Shophar (hallowed ram's horn) in his hand. Instantly the priest covered his head with his *"talate"* (praying shawl) and lifting the horn to his lips he blew "the great Teru-gnah."

Every Jew presently covered his head with his prayer shawl, and the High-Priest, cried:

"Hear, O Israel, the Lord thy God is one God!"

Then turning to the scroll, he read in a curious, monot-onous intone, part of Solomon's prayer at the opening of the Temple:

"Now then, O Lord God of Israel, let Thy word be verified (on the morrow of this day). Thy word which Thou hast spoken unto Thy servant David. Amen."

Inclining his head towards the scroll-bearer, as a sign that he had finished his brief reading, he cleared his voice and addressing his own people, said:

"Brethren, fathers, sons of Father Abraham, Isaac, Jacob, because that the good hand of our God hath been upon us, we are once more restored to our own land. No longer trodden down by stranger's feet, Jerusalem is again for the Jew, and the Jew for Jerusalem. We meet here this afternoon in our own Temple, reared by Jewish gold and patriotism. Our Father's Temple, Solomon's could have been but a poor synagogue compared to this in which we are now found. To-morrow, all the world will be gathered to this place, (all that part of the world worth calling *The* World) to the formal, official opening of this Temple. To-morrow, for the first time since this city, and since "Herod's" Temple were destroyed, we shall slay the morning and evening lamb, the daily sacrifice ordained by our God.

"Today we have an accredited place among the nations. There may be special *Jewish* reasons for the coming to pass of this universal recognition of our race, but chief among the factors that have gone to bring all this about, is the friendship of Lucien Apleon, Emperor, Dictator of the world."

Cohen turned and bowed to the throne where Apleon sat, his face filled with a smile in which pride in his position and quizzical mirth at Cohen's allusion to the soundness of the Jewish position, were mingled.

There was a slight movement among the kings, and other grandees, and amid murmurs of assent at Cohen's allusion to the Emperor, the member of the Royal confederation bowed to the throne.

Cohen proceeded: "In spite of our position, today, fathers and brethren, we could not maintain it a week, and certainly we could not strengthen and consolidate it, but for our Emperor. We desire to maintain, to strengthen our position, hence it has seemed good to the great International Jewish committee to seek to have a covenant wtih Lucien Apleon, Emperor—Dictator of the World. The covenant is for seven years. We on our part are to serve him in every way, he on his part to guarantee our protection—for we have neither Army or Navy—in return for our allegiance to him.

"This covenant, duly drawn up, is here for final signature this afternoon. As your elected High-Priest, and representative of our race, I shall sign it on behalf of our people, our Emperor will also affix his signature.

Then all of us, as a sign of our covenant and our allegiance, will wear a badge which has been prepared. The badge can be worn—like the written Law of our God, as commanded by our father Moses, 'as a sign upon our hand, or as a frontlet between our eyes—.'

"Many millions of the badges have been prepared, made in white metal for *free* distribution to the poorest of the world, or jewelled, gold or silver, for those who would fain purchase something more in accordance with their rank, station, or wealth. The time is at hand when no one will be able to buy or sell, save he who wears this sign."

He paused, and turning to where a little knot of white-robed priests stood, they parted, and showed an exquisite little table of gold and pearl, and on the table a jewelled casket of marvellous workmanship.

Two of the priests bore the table to the centre of the floor where Cohen stood. He opened the casket, drew forth a small silk-tasselled parchment roll, and laid it open upon the table. The two priests held down the curling corners.

A fountain pen—the cylinder of jewelled gold—lay in a hollow of the casket. Cohen took the pen, and wrote at the foot of the text of the covenant:

"In the Name of our God, the God of Abraham, Isaac and Jacob, and on behalf of His chosen people, I Solomon Isaac Cohen (Aaron,) First High-Priest of the new era, in the City of Jerusalem, on the ninth day of September, 19—, (*world's* calculation) subscribe myself."

As he lifted his form erect again, he made a sign to the two priests. They lifted the table and bore it up to the platform of the dais.

Apleon, without rising from the throne, took the pen

and made his signature. Two seals were affixed, Cohen and Apleon, touched them, then the table was once more lifted to the floor level, and the ten kings signed the covenant, *as witnesses.*

Then every one present, save George Bullen, donned one of the badges. In the crowding, his non-compliance was unnoticed. All the kings and most of the princes and others, from Babylon, received massive and costly signet rings from the hands of Apleon, himself, Each signet was engraved with "The *covenant Sign,*" as it was called.

God calls it "The Mark of the Beast."

The recipients of the rings, all wore them on the *third* finger of the right hand, as did others of the minor personages. Many of the Jews, in their enthusiasm, wore one of the "Signs" in the centre of the forehead, held in position by a fine gold chain that passed round the head, as well as one on the right hand.

When the "Covenant" badges had been donned, Apleon was hailed as the world's deliverer, the whole Temple ringing with the plaudits of the kings and others.

A moment, and he passed outside, and stood on the top step of the Temple flight. Again the "Hurrahs" were raised, and caught by the multitudes that thronged that wide marble approach to the gates of the Temple, and caught again and again by ever more distant peoples, until in a moment or two, from three to four million people, inside and outside the city, were belching forth their acclaimings of a demon, counting him almost God.

CHAPTER IX.

THE DEDICATION.

S AVE for the Bible record of the opening of Solomon's Temple, Cohen and his colleague-priests,
had no precedent upon which to base their order of
procedure as regarded the official opening of the Temple,
and the consequent re-commencement and re-establish-
ment of the daily sacrifices.

Then, too, the ideas of the Jew of the period, as
regarded worship, were more or less of a hybrid character, while the modern repugnance to blood-shedding,
and all the consequent unpleasantness of the sacrificial
ceremonies, caused the Jewish leaders to construct a
very much more simple ritual than anything approaching
the original Mosaic standard.

One thing had been decided by them in council, that
was, to make this great epoch in their renationalization
to synchronize with their New Year, which would prop-
erly fall the next month, on October 2nd, to be correct.
The usual New Year's ceremony of Shophar-blowing
would be observed.

Cohen, and his fellow priests, were early at the Temple,
and long before the hour advertised on the programmes
—7-30, every arrangement (from their stand-point) was
complete.

At seven o'clock, sharp, the gun was fired at the
"Palace Apleon," and the great silken flag, with its
"Covenant" sign, flew out upon the breeze. The whole
city and its suburbs were astir.

Suddenly a burst of brazen music rent the more *or* less silent air of the city, and Cohen and his fellow priests knew that the procession had started from the Palace. Soon it was in sight. Oh the wonder, the gorgeousness, the BLASPHEMY of it! Riding on a white horse, there came first the standard bearer. The heel of the standard pole was socketted in a deep barrel of leather that ran from the saddle to the stirrup. The rider was a man of enormous strength, and he had need to be, to bear the strain of the breeze that tugged at the many square yards of white silk, of which the standard was composed. Like the flag on the place, like the brand on the brows and right hands of many of the multitude, the *"Covenant"* sign appeared in the centre of the standard borne aloft by that mounted bearer.

Behind the standard came the band, fifty mounted players. Behind the band there was a gap of sixty or seventy feet. Then, alone, proud, regal, handsome, mighty of stature, noble in pose, mounted on his jet-black mare, and attired as he had been overnight, rode Apleon, the Emperor—Dictator of the World. After him, but with fifty feet of space between, rode the ten kings, then their respective suites. Then came the Babylonian merchant princes, and others.

It was a triumphal procession for Apleon. For it was *his* name that filled throats of the acclaiming multitudes as they roared out their "Huzzahs!"

The scene in the Courtyard of the Temple was one of wondrous pomp, and of even deeper significance. As Apleon rode in, a fan-fare of trumpets gave him greeting. Then when the last intricate brazen note had sounded, the mighty multitude drowned even the memory of the trumpets, by the deafening roar of their Huzzahs!

Ten bugles sounded "Silence." It took a full minute for the command to pass from lip to lip to the uttermost reaches of the people. Then, in the comparative stillness, Apleon dismounted from his horse, took the diamond-studded key from the hand of the High-Priest, opened the door, flung it wide, and proclaimed The Temple opened, "in the name of Apleon, Emperor—Dictator of the World."

That opening word truly translated, meant, "in the name of the Devil, by the person of his Anti-christ."

The High-Priest, standing on the top-step of the wide flight that led to the porch, faced the people and priests, and began to recite selected parts of Solomon's prayer at the Dedication of *his* Temple. These finished, he cried, with a loud voice:

"It having pleased our God to restore us, His chosen earthly people, the Jews, to our own land, and to our own beautiful Zion," joy of the whole earth, "we make the occasion to be as the beginning of a new era, a new year. And as the Lord spake unto Moses and Aaron, in Egypt, saying: 'This month shall be the beginning of months: it shall be the *first month of the year to you,*' so we proclaim to *our* people today, this month shall be the beginning of our New Year, and of a New Dispensation to us."

Dropping his proclamation loudness of voice, he slipped into his synagogue recitative tone, as he went on:

"On the first of the month, shall be a Sabbath, a memorial of blowing of trumpets and holy convocation. Ye shall offer an offering unto the Lord."

He signed to the Tokeang—the Shophar blower—and instantly the weird, curious, quavering, vibrating sounds broke on the still air.

As the last note of the shophar died away, Cohen cried:

"Let all the house of Israel, sacrifice unto the Lord!"

Lifting his hand as he spoke, a turbaned priest led a lamb to the foot of the altar. A gleaming knife, snatched from his girdle flashed for a moment in the air; there was a swift movement of the sacrificial priest's arm, a gurgle from the silent lamb, and the little fleecy thing sank dying upon the grating before the altar.

Only those immediately near could see all that followed, until the moment when the carcass of the lamb was reared to the grating on the summit of the altar.

A strange stillness rested upon the people gathered, as another turbaned priest brought a torch to fire the wood beneath the altar.

Before he could reach the altar, the voice of Apleon stayed his feet.

"Let no fire be brought!" he cried, in commanding tones. "I will consume the offering!"

He stretched his right hand forth, the fingers closed. Then opening his fingers, he drew back his arm suddenly, sharply, then jerked it forward again——it was the old mesmeric pass of the magicians.

Instantly, the interior of the altar blazed with long, fierce forks of many coloured flames, and as they finally resolved themselves into a blood-red fiery cloud that hung over the sacrifice, the *"covenant"* sign floated in white amid the blood-red cloud. Another movement and the red cloud melted away, but like a quivering golden light the "Sign" remained an instant hovering over the altar. When that, too, melted, it was seen that not a vestige of the lamb was left.

Awed and silent, the onlookers wondered! For a moment George Bullen was puzzled. Then he recalled the words of prophecy, as regarded The Anti-christ.

"His coming is after the working of Satan, with all power and signs and lying wonders . . . . And he doeth great wonders, so that he maketh fire come down from heaven on the earth in the sight of men, and deceiveth them that dwell on the earth by the means of those miracles which he had power to do."

The greatest tribute that could have been given to the supernatural power exhibited by Apleon, was the awed silence, and the bowed heads of all who had witnessed his satanic miracle.

Its effect upon Cohen and the rest of the Jews, was, if possible, greater than upon any of the Gentiles who had witnessed the wonder.

Upon the awed silence there suddenly fell a deep growl of thunder. The startled people lifted their heads. With almost an instantaneousness, the heavens darkened. It might well have been a moonless midnight, so dark did it suddenly become.

The thunders roared and cannonaded, while fierce lightnings, like liquid fires, raced earthwards down the blackened heavens. No one, native of the land, or foreigner, had ever known thunder or lightning such as now broke upon them.

For days afterwards men were as deaf as though born thus, stunned by the thunder; and scores lost their sight from the lightning's flash, never to recover it again.

As sudden as the darkness, there now came a hurricane blast that tore at the Temple walls as if it would hurl its gold and marbles into the valley below. No man could keep his footing in the courtyard or on that summit, and everyone flung themselves prone to the earth—save Apleon. He stood smiling his sardonic, contemptuous smile.

Cohen and a few others crawled towards the wide, folding-doors of the Temple. But the hurricane was before them, and the doors slammed to, and, in some way jammed.

The horses started in stampede, terrified by the storm. Apleon spoke the one word "Soh!" and they stood absolutely still, save for a long, shuddering kind of shiver that ran through each beast at the same instant.

Now, for a few minutes, the thunder roared louder and deeper, until it drowned the thunderous roar of the wind. Peal followed peal with hideous, horrible swiftness. The lightning was a succession of fierce, white ribbons of blood-red flaming fire.

For ten minutes this extraordinary storm raged. There was not one drop of rain. Then, with a suddenness only equalled by that of the starting of the storm, it ceased. The blackness of the heavens rolled away like mist before the rising sun, and while all the western horizon suddenly glowed with the fierce red glow of a furnace blaze, the sun appeared once more over-head shining as though nought had happened.

The procession now re-formed, in the order in which it had arrived, and to the lilt of the gay music of the powerful band, the volatile spirits of the multitude revived, and the loud "huzzahs" rent the air as Apleon— the Anti-christ—passed through the waiting masses of the people.

George Bullen contrived to keep Apleon full in view. In a general way no item of the procession of the cere-

mony at the Temple, or of aught else had escaped him—
but it was *in*, and *on* Apleon that his special attention had
been concentrated.

He watched the procession sweep through the great
gate-way of the Emperor's Palace. Then, when the last
of the guests had passed in, the huge folding gates closed,
and the multitudes began to disperse.

The vast bulk of the pepole were lodged *out*side the
city, and now poured out through the gates—for, with
the practical re-building of the city, the exits had been
made very numerous.

Bullen was lodging with a Christian Syrian about
half-a-mile outside the city. He moved on in a line with
one of the exodus streams.

As he cleared the city, he became conscious that just
ahead of him there was a great and ever increasing gathering of people—a mighty throng, in fact. Arriving at
the fringe of the crowd which grew closer and closer,
as well as greater, every moment, he was amazed to see
two very striking looking Easterns, clothed in sackcloth,
and standing high upon a mound of stone. The appearance of the two men was extraordinary. The face of the
elder of the two was cast in a wonderful mould.

George Bullen was fairly well versed in the facial
characteristics of all the known races—*past* as well as
present. But this man's face bore no relation to any
type he had ever seen depicted. Eastern, it was, it is
true, but unlike, and more beautiful than anything he
knew of. The calm of it was wondrous, and George
involuntarily found himself saying over: "Thou wilt
keep him in *perfect peace* whose mind is stayed on Thee,"
and instantly there flashed upon him, in connection with

that word, one other: Enoch *walked with God,* and was not, for God took him."

"He might be Enoch returned to earth," he told himself.

The other man was a different specimen. His features were strongly Jewish marked. There was a fierceness of eye, a power for a blazing wrath in his deep-set orbs. Not that the first man's eyes and face were incapable of fiery indignation, but they gave indication of having been schooled by long intercourse with the divine keeping power of the God of Peace.

The men were evidently preachers—prophet-preachers. They spoke alternately, their voices clear, far-reaching, their tones perfectly natural—there was no raising of the voice—yet reaching as far as the farthest listener.

Their message was a Testimony to God, to His power, His might, His Holiness, even to His mercy. They told of judgments, near at hand, upon all who would not cleave to God in righteousness. Then in deeply solemn tones, they spoke of the presence of the "Mark of the Beast," upon the persons of so many thousands of the people, and warned all who would not discard the badge, and throw over their allegiance to Apleon,—"The Antichrist—that they would presently share in the awful destruction which should overtake Anti-christ and his followers."

A roar, savage and full as from ten thousand lions with the snarl of wolves in it, greeted this last part of the testimony, while a thousand throats belched forth the cry:

"Down with them! murder them!"

There was a savage rush towards the sackclothed prophets. But though the multitude of would-be murderers swept over, around, and past the mound on which the two faithful witnesses had been standing, and though they did not *see* them disappear, yet they were not found.

"And when they shall have completed their Testimony, the Beast that cometh up out of the abyss shall make war with them, and overcome them, and kill them—."

"Yes," mused George Bullen, "when they have completed their Testimony," and not an hour, or a day before. For these are evidently God's two faithful witnesses, Enoch and Elijah, the only two men who never passed through mortal death, and hence are the only two saints who can become God's witnesses, in this hideous Anti-christ time, for, as witnesses, they must be slain in the streets of the city of Jerusalem—*"where also their Lord was crucified."*

There was much angry talk, and savage swearing among the enraged, mystified, disappointed multitude, at the loss of their vengeance upon the witnesses, but, had they known it, they had come off very lightly in being only disappointed, for God's witnesses had the power *"when any one willed to injure them, to send forth fire out of their mouths, and to devour their enemies,"* and in the days that were to follow this first encounter with them, the multitude would learn this to their cost.

CHAPTER X.

A LEBANON ROSE.

WITH the disappearance of the two witnesses there came a gradual darkening of the heavens, until in the space of a couple of minutes, the whole district became as dark as it had been when the sacrifice in the Temple courtyard had finished.

Thunder and lightning accompanied the darkness, and this time heavy rain. Baffled by the darkness, the multitude ran hither and thither, aimlessly, wildly, in search of their homes. Presently the vivid lightning flashes gave them fitful direction, and gradually the crowds melted away.

George Bullen had swerved from his homeward way, to reach the crowd about the "two witnesses." The gleaming lightning gave him his direction now. He was already drenched to the skin, for the rain was a deluge.

As he moved on through the black darkness, (illumined only with the occasional lightning flashes) he stumbled over something. Some instinct told him it was a human form. Stooping in the blackness, and groping with his hands, he made out that the form was that of a slender woman. There was no movement, and in response to his question, "are you hurt?" there came no reply.

The face, the lips which he touched with his groping fingers, were warm, so that he knew it was not death, though the form was as still as death.

"Whoever she is," he mused, "she will die in this storm if she is left here." So he stooped and gathered the drenched form up in his arms. Her head fell upon his breast, her limbs were nerveless in his clasp.

Another, a longer, a more vivid flash of lightning, came at this instant, and showed him his path clearly. He was close to his lodgings.

Two minutes later he had reached the door of the house. It was on the latch, and he entered with his burden. He found his way to his room, laid the warm, breathing form down upon a rug upon the floor, and lit the lamp.

By the light of the lamp he saw that the poor soul he had rescued, was a sweet-faced Syrian girl, by whose side he had found himself standing on the evening before, when he had stood in the throng on the Temple mount. They had exchanged a few words of ordinary tourist-interchange, and he had been surprised to find that she could speak good English, though with a foreign accent.

But realizing now that she needed immediate attention, if she was to be saved from taking a chill, he lit a tiny hand-lamp and carrying it with him to light his way, he went in search of the woman of the house.

As recorded on an earlier page, the people with whom he had found lodgment were Christian Syrians—a husband and wife.

He went all over the premises, but though he shouted several times, neither the husband or wife answered or appeared. There was no sign of them anywhere.

"They were probably caught, as I was, in the storm," he told himself, as he returned to where he had left the rain-soaked Syrian girl.

He had a bottle of mixture, which he always carried on Eastern travel, as a preventive of chill. He poured

out a little of the warming stuff, and raising the unconscious girl he poured a few drops through her parted
lips.

She drank by mere instinct. He repeated the experi-
ment, and she caught her breath sharply as she swallowed
the second draught. A faint sigh escaped her, her eye-
lids trembled, and, a moment more they unclosed.

At first her gaze was unseeing, then slowly she took
in his anxious face. "Where—am—I?" she murmured
brokenly.

"You are safe, and with friends!" he replied. "I
stumbled over you in the road, you had fallen, somehow, in that dreadful thunder-storm."

Her eyes met his, and for one long instant she seemed
to be searching his face. Then a weak, little smile
trembled about her mouth, as she said:

"We met last night—I remember I thought how *true*
your face was—I can trust you, I know."

A sigh, more of content than aught else, escaped her,
and he felt how she let herself rest more fully in his
supporting arm. He gave her another sip of the cordial,
and she thanked him as some sweet child might have
done.

For a moment she lay silent and still, then she spoke
again, in a vague, speculative way, as though she was
searching her mind for the clue:

"Ah, yes, I remember now. The great darkness came
on, after those good men of God had spoken. And the
crowd got frightened and ran hither and thither,—to find
their homes, I suppose—and in the darkness some rushed
against me, knocked me down, and—and—"

She shuddered, as she added, "I believe some others
kicked me and trampled upon me, and—"

"Are you hurt?" he cried anxiously. "Do you feel as if any bone was broken, anywhere?"

She smiled back into his anxious face: "Hurt? not much! Certainly no bones are broken. But I feel bruised and sore, and—so—"

She shivered, as she added: "so cold!"

He awoke to the immediate necessity for her to get out of her wet clothes, and gently lifting her until she stood upon her feet, he said:

"Can you stand alone, do you think?"

"Let go your hold," she answered, " and I will see."

Very reluctantly George released his hold of her, though his eyes were anxious, and his hands were stretched out within reach of her, lest she should give way.

She put her hand to her head, as she said: "I feel a little dizzy, but that will pass off."

"When did you eat anything last?" he inquired.

"Oh, I had a good breakfast, before I started out this morning. If I could lie down somewhere,—and sleep—for I slept but badly last night—I think I should soon be all right."

He explained that he could not find the man or wife of the house, but, (pointing to a room beyond) he said:

"There is a bed there, and there are female clothes hanging in a recess (they were there when I occupied the room) go in there, dear child."

She seemed but a child, to him, so sweet and innocent was her face.

"Divest yourself of every rag of your wet clothes (drop them out of the window, and I will gather them up, and get them dry for you) chafe yourself with the towels you will find in the room, then wrap yourself in one of the sheets or rugs, and try and sleep."

"Ah, kind friend! How good you are!" she said, softly, a deep sense of what she owed him, (for he had doubtless, she realized, saved her life) moving her heart strangely.

With the shy, tender grace of a child, she caught his hand and kissed it, leaving two great warm teardrops upon it, as she cried:

"May God reward you! You saved my life!"

Her long silken lashes held great quivering drops upon them. Her hair—what swathes there were of it —had become loosened, and hung about her in long, thick, wet tresses. Her cheeks were warmed to a vivid tinting by the cordial, the excitement by the deep emotion that filled her, so that, in that moment she looked very beautiful.

He led her to the room he had indicated, and glancing around to see that the towels were in the place, he said, "what is your name?"

"In English?" she asked. Then without waiting for him to reply, added: "Rose!"

"Mine is George!" he returned. Then with a final word of: "Sleep, if you can!" he left her.

When the hanging over the door-way had dropped behind him, and he was alone in his little living room, he tried to think out the many wonderful things that had happened since he had sallied forth at half-past six that morning.

Taking his note-book from his breast, he tore the sheaf of short-hand notes he had already made, along the perforated line, and began to compose his message for the "Courier" in the code that had been previously arranged.

It took him an hour and a half to complete the work, as writing in code, took longer than the ordinary method.

By the time he had finished, it was past noon, and he wondered at the stillness of the house. Once more he made a tour of the other part of the premises, calling the names of both the man and woman of the house.

They were still absent. It was very mysterious! He could not know that they were among the scores of those who had been trampled to death in the horrible darkness on the Temple mount that morning.

Passing back to his room, he listened at the hanging over that inner room, where the rescued girl lay. He could hear her softly, regularly snoring, and decided to get his message off while she slept.

He was a little dubious about leaving the house door unlocked, yet feared to lock it lest the man and wife should return.

He was gone an hour. Both going and returning, he had been struck with the general desertedness of the streets, but realized that in all probability every one would be resting after the scenes of the morning.

Entering the house he found it exactly as he had left it, and beginning to feel hungry, he hunted about for the wherewithal to make a meal.

Deciding that his *protege* might soon be stirring, he carried into his living-room all the materials for a meal. When he had spread his table, he remembered the clothes for his *protege* (he had spread them in the sun to dry, having found them where she had dropped them, by his instructions, out of the window.)

Passing quietly back to the hanging between the two rooms, he listened again. This time she was awake and

softly humming the air of "The sands of Time are sink-
ing."

Lifting the hanging a few inches at the bottom he
thrust the clothes underneath, and called:

"Do you feel well enough to get up, Rose? If you do,
I will make coffee, and we will have a meal!"

"Thank you, thank you, good George!" she cried, with
the *naivete* of an innocent child. "I will dress and come
out, for oh, I am so hungry and thirsty!"

He smiled to himself at her sweet child-likeness, and
hurried away to make the coffee.

Whether the aroma of the coffee reached her senses
and hurried her, it would be impossible to say, but certainly, in an incredibly short space of time (for a
woman) she drew aside the hanging a little, and asked:
"May I come, please?"

He flung aside the hanging, his smile, as well as his
voice saying: "Come!"

Then as she appeared before him, bright, fresh from
her sound restful sleep, her hair carefully groomed and
coiled in a crown on her head, her cheek glowing with
the prettiest, tenderest blushes, he thought how beautiful
she was!

A woman, evidently, in years, (as she would be judged
in the east) yet a pure child in character and manner.

"How do you feel little Rose?" he asked, taking her
hand in greeting.

"A little stiff," she answered, "but that is more from
the bruises than ought else, I think, for—"

Her cheeks warmed to a deeper tint, as she said:

"I have a dozen or more bruises!"

"Let us sit down," he laughed, "and we can do two
things at once, eat and talk."

Half an hour passed; they ate and drank, and grew almost merry as they exchanged a few notes. When, however, in response to her question:

"But you are English, George?" he replied.

"Yes! Though as I speak Syrian perfectly, and Hebrew fairly, it seems better for me not to appear to be English, hence my Syrian costume. I feel I can trust you, Rose, my new little friend, so I do not mind telling you that I belong to a great English newspaper, and as many of those *now* in authority are opposed to our paper, I am passing as a Syrian, that I may better get my reports, for our paper, through to England."

She had started when he began to speak of his connection with a great English Newspaper. Now she interrupted him, saying, in a cautious whisper:

"Are you Mr. Ralph Bastin?"

It was his turn to start now, and in amaze, he cried:

"No, I am not Ralph Bastin, but I *am* his representative. But——"

His voice grew hoarse with excitement, as he added, low and cautiously:

"What do you know about Ralph Bastin?"

She glanced frightenedly around, then with her finger raised, she whispered:

"The very air seems full of spies here, as it was at Babylon."

She leant towards him until her lips almost touched his ear, and whispered:

"Lucien Apleon, The Emperor, has decreed that Ralph Bastin is to be slain!"

"Tell me more, Rose, trust me absolutely, dear child!" His voice was very hoarse as he spoke.

"How do you know this?" he added. "But perhaps you had better tell me who and what you are, dear child!"

He leant to her that his voice might be a whisper only, for he realized her warning of a moment ago. "Do not fear, dear child, I shall hold as sacred as my faith in God, anything that you tell me!"

She laid her pretty little plump hand in his, and looked at him confidingly out of her great Eastern liquid eyes, as with a beaming smile, she said:

"I could not be afraid of you, good George, you saved my life, and——"

She sighed, and there was a sound of supreme content this time in the sigh. "No," she went on, "I could not be afraid of you, my saviour from death. And I can, I will, confide in you, for I sorely need a friend, and I feel, I know I can trust you. I had been asking God, yesterday, to help me, to guide me to a friend, and I feel that He has sent you into my life at this point when I, a lone girl, need most a friend. Someday I may be able to tell you all the story of my life. It will be enough here, however, to tell you that, for two months, I have been in Babylon, with my brother—my only living relative, as far as I know. Babylon——"

She shuddered as she repeated the name, and her face flushed scarlet, then paled as swiftly, while a look of horror leaped into her eyes, and she gazed fearfully round as though she feared some terror of the foul and mighty city might even here have pursued her.

"No tognue dare, no tongue *can* tell a thousandth part of the abominations of that sink of iniquity. I came here with my brother three days ago, and he has joined hands with "The People of the Mark." He is clever, very clever! They know that, and because he will be useful to them, he has been placed in high office among them, and——"

She paused abruptly, and with another frightened glance around, whispered:

"Do you know what 'the mark' is, and what it means?"

"Is it what has been flying over the 'Eternal City' here, in the centre of that great white flag that floats over the Apleon Palace? I think you must mean that, and if so it is the two Greek characters for the name of Christ, with a crooked serpent put between them!"

"Yes!" the one word came in merest whisper from her, then leaning closer to him, she went on:

"But do you know, George, the *import* of the foul Mark?"

"I believe I do!" he whispered back. I believe it is what our Scriptures call the 'Mark of the Beast.' If that be so, as I am convinced it is, it is the brand of the Anti-christ—and——"

He, too, seemed to feel the need of increased caution, for he glanced fearsomely round, as he added:

"And I believe I know who the Anti-christ will prove to be."

She shot a swift glance upwards to the casement window, and with upraised finger, leant towards him until her warm lips touched his ear, as she repeated what she had said once before:

"The very air here, seems full of spies. It was so at Babylon! *Lucien Apleon* IS THE ANTI-CHRIST."

Again her frightened glance travelled to the casement. Then she went on:

"My brother always confided everything to me. And in telling me the secret of the Emperor Apleon—though exactly how he learned it, I cannot say—he never dreamed that I should have any scruples about serving the Anti-christ. But I love God! I missed the great 'Rapture,' when God's true children were taken 'into the air' with their Lord, but, though it cost me torture, or my very life, during these coming days of awful perse-cution, I can do no other than cleave to our Lord."

In an unconscious gesture of loyalty to her God, she had drawn herself up to her full height, while her vow of fidelity had been uttered aloud.

For awhile longer they talked on together of Babylon, of "The Mark," of Anti-christ, of the probable coming days of horror and persecution, then a chance question of his as to how she came to learn to speak English so well, led her to say:

"Shall I tell you my story? The sun is too hot for you to go out for another two hours, and——"

"Yes, tell me, Rose," he cried, not giving her time to finish her sentence.

He glanced towards a low Eastern couch on the other side of the room, as he added: "But before you begin, I want to see you lying upon that couch; after all you have passed through, and in view of unexpected con-tingencies that may arise, any hour, you must rest all that you can."

He made her comfortable, with cushions, on the couch, then seating himself cross-legged on the floor by her side—the posture was a favorite one of his, and had been acquired, long ago, during his residence in the East —he bade her go on.

"I was born," she began, "in a little village at the foot of Lebanon, but when I was only six years old my father got work in the neighbourhood of Trebizond, and we migrated thither. Within a week of our arrival, at our new home, I became a scholar in a lady Missionary's class of native children, where, among other things, I learned English. When I was eleven, my father and mother died of small-pox, and I became a little waiting-maid to my dear American missionary teacher, Miss Roosevelly, living in the house, with her, of course.

"My brother Hassan, was eight years older than me, and he lived with a schoolmaster, in Constantinople. I had also a dear old grandmother, my mother's mother, who lived about four miles from the tiny mission where I lived, and, now and again, I was allowed to visit grand-mother for two or three days at a time.

"My life was an even, regular, but never montonous one, for I was always busy. Then, a year or more ago, there came an awful event in my life. I was sixteen, and I had gone to spend a few days with dear old grand-mother, and——"

There came the faintest click in her voice, and she glanced toward the lemonade caraffe. His watching eyes saw her need, and he reached the caraffe and a glass, and poured out a draught. She took a big gulp, then sipped more slowly. And while she drank, he watched her and he realized more than ever, how true and sweet as well as how beautiful her face was.

Young as she was, in development she was a woman, as is invariably the case of maidens born under tropical skies. It is true that her beauty was, as yet, of the tender, budding type, but it was the full bursting bud of the queen of flowers, and already foreshadowed the wondrous brilliance of the full-blown blossom.

Eastern though she was, she had blue eyes—forget-me-not-blue—though the long silken eye-lashes, and the thin, arched, pencilled-like eye-brows were raven black.

When she had finished her lemonade, and had replaced the glass on the table, she went on with her story.

"It was the first evening of my home-coming to dear grandmother. The sun was setting, and the roseate gold of his departing glory was illuminating everything. How lovely it all was! The gold of that sunset—I shall never wholly forget it, I think—was everywhere. It glittered among the tree-tops, gilded the hill-crests, changed the eastern horizon into a molten sea of warmest gold and colour; and——"

"Transfigured Rose, eh," he broke in, with a smile.

She laughed merrily as she said: "I am afraid I was forgetting myself, talking so much description!"

A shadow passed over her face, as she went on:

"How quickly everything was to be changed, though! Grandmother's voice called me from inside, Come, Rose, my child, and we will give God our evening chant!

"I am afraid I sighed, as I turned from watching all that sunset loveliness. It was not that I disliked our evening devotions, but somehow felt *that* evening—as I have often done, in fact—that I would fain worship God with all His evening miracle before my eyes, and would fain then have lingered on in the glorious after-glow, though that after-glow lasted all too short a time.

"I turned into the house, but I did not close the door, for it would have seemed like sacrilege to have shut out all that glory. I took my place by grandmother's side, with my hands folded across my breast, as, together, we chanted 'Our Father who art in Heaven! Hallowed be Thy name.'

"How it all remains with me, and ever will, all the little items of that last night of dear grandma's life! I can seem to hear her voice even now, she was very old, and it quavered and quivered like one of our hill-country dulcimers!

"Our chant over, grandmother prayed, she prayed extra long that night and our quick night had come down before she had finished. I lit a little lamp, and we went to bed. Then——"

A shudder passed through her beautiful, reclining frame, as she continued, and her voice had a new note in it, a note of pain:

"It was about midnight. The whole country slept. There were sixteen small houses in our little village. They all huddled close together, (for once there had been a wall enclosing them) suddenly there was a sound of gun-fire. I leaped from my bed—Ah, me! I cannot describe it. In half-an-hour the awful tragedy was completed. Every old man and woman was killed, slain with a sword, or hacked to death, or speared. Babies, and little children were brained against the walls of the houses; strong men—fathers, lovers, sons—had been murdered with every wantonness of savagery conceivable. The only persons spared had been the budding girls, and one or two of the best looking of the women.

"Everything of value, that was readily portable, had been seized, each raider keeping his own lootings. Then, at last, at a given signal, the murderers and robbers reformed themselves into a solid company, and rode away, setting fire to the village in half-a-dozen separate places before they left.

"I was, of course, one of the girls whose life had been spared. The man who had seized upon me, when, in my fright, I had run from my bed to the cottage door, had flashed the light of a torch upon me, and even now I can recall the fierce delight and satisfaction that leaped

into his greedy eyes, and the manner of his mutterings:
"Good! Good! She'll *sell* well!"

"He stood over me while I dressed warmly, then hurried me out into the open again. Grandmother had made
no sound, given no sign of waking, and I wondered. I
wanted to go into the little room where her bed was, but
my captor would not let me—I never saw her again,
and can only fear that, if God had not already taken her
in her sleep (and sometimes I think this must have been
the case), she was slain with the rest of the old
people.

"Of the next week I have no distinct remembrance. I
believe I travelled, travelled, travelled, ate, drank, slept,
but all my faculties seemed numbed, and my mind was
largely a blank. It was when I was being taken into
Constantinople, that I began to arouse from my strange
mental and physical stupor.

"It was through the cool mist of the morning that I
got my first glimpse of the city of which I had heard so
much. Santa Sophia, rising like some beautiful dream-
structure, with the points of its four light, airy, minarets
flashing in the sunlight. Then, little by little, kiosks, tall
sad-looking cypresses, sycamores, and the other thou-
sand-and-one wonders of that city of beautiful and
revolting contradictions, took shape and form.

"By seven o'clock we were in the heart of the city,
and breakfasting. My captor had treated me with a certain rough kindness through all the journey, and done
his best to hearten me. He had told me my fate—to be
sold into a harem—but he had pictured it as glowingly,
as glitteringly as his rough eloquence would let him.
And, with all the blood of countless centuries of Eastern
races coursing in my veins, and in the more or less stun-

ned, stupified condition in which that awful night-tragedy
had left me, I yielded, for the time, to the fatalism with
which we Easterns are familiarized from our babyhood.

"My captor was no novice at the business of selling a
girl, neither was he a stranger to the house to which he
had taken me. For, after breakfast, he showed me into
a little room with one quaint, Arabesque window. In
this room there was a bath, and every toilette requisite,
while, from a tin box that he brought in, he took out a
number of most exquisite outer and under garments.
Telling me to make myself as beautiful-looking as I
knew how, he presently left me.

"I am afraid that for a time I was too overwhelmed
to do more than weep. Then as I remembered that it
would be the worse for me if I angered my master, I
bathed and anointed myself, though I remember how
once I paused, as I scented my body, and said, through
my blinding tears: 'This is like preparing myself for a
sacrificial altar.'

"I was sitting an hour later, on an ottoman in the
room outside the bath-room, when I heard voices, and
steps, and a moment later my master, accompanied by a
little tub of a man, with fatted-hog kind of face, greasy-
looking, and wrinkled with fat, out of which peered two
tiny black eyes—like currants stuck in a bladder of lard
—and twinkling most villainously, entered the room.

"He was very richly dressed, and bore the name of
Osman Mahmed, and, as I afterwards learned, he was
very high in office and in favour with the Sultan. He
was fabulously rich, and, excepting the Sultan, had the
most extensive harem in the city.

"I had, as a child, learned the Turkish tongue, and
had no difficulty in following all that passed between the

seller and buyer. Then after being lightly pinched, pressed, and squeezed, and ogled, the bargain was struck, the money for my purchase was paid, and my captor was instructed to take me, veiled, to the purchaser's palace at two o'clock that afternoon.

"I was taken, as arranged, to the Palace, and given in charge of the head eunuch. A few minutes later, two female slaves took me to a large dressing-room. Here I was bathed again, and sprayed with a very valuable perfume, a curious blending of rose and patchouli.

"I have three crosses tatooed on my body. Each cross consists of eleven blue dots, one on each of my shoulders, and one on my breast, and I noticed a look of horror come into the faces of the two slave-women who were attending me, but neither of them asked any question of me.

"My hair was well-groomed, and beautifully dressed, and strings of gold sequins, and glittering jewelled stars were twisted amid the swathes of my hair. Then came my robing in garments, so rich, so wonderful, that they almost took my breath away. When the very last touch had been given to this wonderful toilette, one of the attendants gave me a *cachou* from a box to sweeten my breath.

"Then, for a time, I was left alone, a strange and awful fear of some coming evil stealing over me. For I could not forget the looks of fear and of terror of the slave-women, at the sight of the crosses on my arms and breast.

"Wondering what type of place I was in, I got up and looked out of the casement. A marble court lay just below the window, and, in the centre of the court was a most beautiful marble basin, quite twenty feet across, from the heart of which there rose a fountain, with a graceful *jet d' eau,* flinging its spray high in the air. Two flights of balustraded steps led down into the basin, a few white doves fluttered about the steps. Flower borders and beds were artistically dotted about the court; and cool-looking, shady bowers clung to the high walls like swallow-nests to the house-eaves.

"But the beauty of all I saw could not drive from me the strange sense of dread of some coming disaster. Suddenly, a huge Sudanese eunuch appeared, and signed for me to follow him; and a minute later I was ushered into a room where the chief eunuch, and that hideous little tub of a Vizier, who had bought me, were.

"The fat, greasy face was distorted with rage, the eyes were blood-shot and fierce, and his voice was almost a scream, as he cried out to me:

" 'What is this they tell me of you, you Lebanon beast? Are you one of those dogs, the Christians?'

" 'I am!' I replied.

"The fat little beast on the dais spat at me, the foul expectoration falling short of my robe by barely a foot.

" 'Your body, the body I bought,' he yelled, 'is damned by the cursed sign of the cross, they tell me.'

"I gave him no reply, and he yelled, 'I will see for myself.' Then to the two eunuchs, he yelled: 'Strip her!'

"The men did his bidding, and nude, and shamed, I stood before that foul tyrant.

" 'Bring her closer!' he yelled, and the big Soudanese lifted me bodily, and dropped me upon my feet on a mat not a yard from the Vizier.

"He glared at the tatooed cross upon my breast, then with a fearful curse, he spat full into my breast, the vileness running down the sacred sign. Then, as a

fiendish look filled his face, he ordered the chief eunuch
to send me for sale in any market that would be open
for such carrion.

"At a word from the chief eunuch, the big Soudanese snatched me up in his brawny hands, tucked me
under his arm, as a father might laughingly carry his
five-year-old boy, and bore me off.

"The rest of the story is all too wonderful for more
than the merest outline. I was being taken through the
streets, veiled, of course, to a dealer in girls, when suddenly I saw my brother Hassan, coming towards me. My
veil, of course, would prevent his knowing me, but tearing off my veil, I leaped towards him, crying:

"Hassan, Hassan, save me!"

She paused in her recital, her voice choked with deep
emotion for a moment, then, as she recovered herself,
she went on:

" 'How wonderful are God's providences! His ways
are past finding out!'

"Hassan was walking—when I met him—with an
officer of the American Embassy—Hassan was clerking
for this officer—and though the eunuch tried to make a
fuss, when he knew who the officer was, he scuttled back
to the Palace as hard as he could go.

"That night, Hassan and I left the city, lest there
should be any attempt to seize me, and—"

She paused suddenly, and he leaped to his feet at the
same instant, for, from the direction of the city, there
came sounds of loud and prolonged hurrahing.

"I will go out and see what is going on!" he said.
"Perhaps," he added, "in these disturbed times, it would
be well for you to fasten the doors, while I am gone.
Whether the people of the house or I, return first, you

can easily ascertain who it is, before you open. Meanwhile, find your way to the other parts of the house, and make yourself coffee or anything else that you may need —and,"

He held out his hand—: "Good bye, for the present, and, another time, you must tell me the rest of your wonderful story, and especially how it came about that you knew so much of Christianity and yet did not share in the 'Rapture' of Christ's own."

With the warmth of her Southern, Eastern nature, remembering how he had saved her, she lifted the hand he gave her, to her lips, and kissed it passionately, leaving two heavy tear-drops on it, when she dropped it.

A moment later she was alone. She had barred the outer doors, when he left.

CHAPTER XI.

HERO-WORSHIP.

NEITHER George Bullen, or the "Lebanon Rose," whom he had so opportunely saved, had had any idea of how rapidly time had fled during that afternoon. On reaching the street, and looking at his watch, George was amazed to find that it was past six o'clock. Moving as briskly as it was wise to do, so as not to call attention to himself, he made his way to where the noise of the multitude told him that something extra was happening.

He soon discovered that the excitement came from a kind of impromptu mass meeting that had followed upon the appearance of Apleon riding on his now celebrated black charger.

The first thing which struck Bullen was the fact that, already, *every* one seemed to be wearing the "Covenant" sign—"The Mark of the Beast." He himself appeared to be the only person who was not wearing it. And—was it fancy? or did Apleon's eyes fix on him with a momentary scowl.

The second thing which struck him, was the intense admiration and homage of the great crowd—all classes alike seemed absolutely infatuated—for this Emperor-Dictator of the world, Lucien Apleon, "The Anti-christ."

Two cries rose loud and laudatory from the multitude "Who is like Apleon? Who dare oppose him?" It was the utimate fruit of the jingoism of the previous years!

"This is what John beheld," Bullen told himself, "*all*

the world wondered after the Beast!" They are, already, worshipping him, in their poor deluded hearts, as a God!

Almost, it seemed to the young journalist as though there was headed up in this one man—the Man of Sin— all that men through the by-gone ages had worshipped. The captivating power of ancient Babylon. The mighty prowess of the Medo-Persian, the power that held all the world in subjection and awe. The Grecian polish. The Roman legal acumen, and martial perfection. All these things seemed combined in this one notable man. And added to all this, there was his resistless attractiveness, his beauty of face, his grace of form, his wondrous voice, his regal air—*"all the world wondered after him."*

As, after awhile, he walked slowly homewards, George Bullen asked himself the question:

"How can it have come to pass, that in comparatively so short a time, it should be possible for all the world to be ready to yield an almost idolatrous obedience to one man?"

Unconsciously to himself his pace slackened, it was as though his mind had willed to have time to review things that should answer his question, before he should reach his rooms, and the consideration should be broken into.

"There was first," he mused "that gradual falling away from the Truth of God, for a full half of the nineteenth century—very gradual, very slow, and very subtle at first, but growing bolder each year, until, in the early part of the first decade of the twentieth century, men calling themselves Christians, taking the salaries of Christian ministers, openly denied every fundamental truth of the Bible—Sin, the Fall, The Atonement, The Resurrection, the Immaculate Birth of Christ, His Deity, the Personality of Satan, the Personality of The Holy

Spirit, and everything else in God's word which clashed with the flesh of their unregenerate lives.

"Then there was the giving heed to seducing spirits *and teachings of demons* (demonology, called spiritism) *'forbidding to marry'* (doctrine of Lust, known as 'Free Love.')

"Great forces were at work during the latter part of the nineteenth century, and more especially in the early part of the twentieth, all of which were preparing the way for the Anti-christ.

"What blinded intellects called 'Progress,' was really Apostasy. And Scientists, Materialists, and Humanists, and the *world's* teachers were all looking for some great outstanding genius, some super-man.

"The Believing Church, before the 'Rapture,' had its Hope, a Hope given by God of *A Man* who should head all things up in Himself, and clothe His Church with His own glory. And that Man came, the Man Christ Jesus, the Lord of Glory. And all the time the world had *its* hope, and just as Christ, the Hope of the Church, said *'I will come again,'* so He also said, as regards the world's hope, *'Another shall come in his own name,'* and now—"

George Bullen paused in his walking and looked back to where the laudatory shouts of the deluded multitude, still rose around Apleon.

"And now," he continued, "that other *has* come, come in his own name, and the world has received him. As late as nineteen hundred and eight, one of the world's so-called 'great thinkers,' a D.D., too, said:

" 'We still wait for *The Genius* who shall state our fundamental faith in accordance with that insight which the *modern man* has gained.'

"That *great thinker*,' if he is living, ought now to be satisfied, for his *'Genius'* has appeared. And if he still possesses a Bible, let him turn to Revelation, thirteen-eighteen, and he will know how all his fancied man-progress was prophesied for nearly two thousand years ago in the words: *'Here is wisdom. Let him that hath understanding count the number of the beast; for it is* THE NUMBER OF MAN; *and his number is 666.'*

"Oh, yes, in a hundred and one ways, the coming of the Anti-christ, and the consequent worship of his Satanic-energized personality, was well-paved; for the world relegated to the limbo of the past, God's evangel as effete, superstitious, worn-out, and it was then prepared for the Devil's lie, the Great Delusion."

By this time George's feet had carried him to the door of the house. He knocked, as arranged before leaving, three slow, deliberate knocks and two others, sharp, quickly-following.

Almost instantly Rose appeared at the door. She had prepared an evening meal, and over the supper-table he told her all that he had seen and heard, while out, adding:

"The whole world will be abjectly at the feet of that man of Satan, presently."

For a few moments they talked on together, then she rose to clear the table. His eyes followed her in all her movements, for, in spite of her bruised stiffness, all that she did was done so deftly, and every movement of her beautiful form was full of the grace of perfect ease.

Now, almost for the first time, it came to him with full seriousness, "What am I to do with her? since, saving her, housing her I have, to a certain extent, made myself responsible for her?"

When she returned to the room, after clearing the last thing from the table, he said:

"We must face your future, Rose! What are your plans, or haven't you any?"

"I am afraid I have no plans," she returned. "You see, good George, I was so terrified at all I heard from my brother, that I simply got away as quickly as I could, without any plan for the future, other than that there has always been, at the back of my mind, an idea, that should I ever (from any cause whatever) become a refugee, I should make my way to England. For, rightly or wrongly; I believe the peoples of all the world have always associated with England the two thoughts of safety and liberty."

Lifting her eyes to his, a bright smile filling all her face, she went on:

"I am not without money. I have nearly twenty-five pounds with me. The question is, where would one— who would rather die than wear the 'Mark of the Beast' —be safest? In England, do you think?"

"I don't know, Rose. *My* place is there, because my *duty* lies there. And now that I have, I think, finished all that I can do here, I ought to be getting back, at once. I ought, I think, to go to-night. At ten-thirty there is a good service to the West, but I cannot leave you alone here. I fear that death, in some way, must have overtaken the people of this house, so that I cannot remain here, but must leave the house to its fate. But about you, Rose? I cannot leave you, like the house, to your fate!"

With the absolute trust of a little child, she stretched her hands towards him, saying:

"Good George, my saviour already from one dreadful death, save me again please. Take care of me until we get to England, take me with you, I will be no expense to you, I will give no trouble, I will—"

Her clinging, child-like trust moved him greatly. He took the two pretty, plump little hands in his, and holding them in a clasp, firm and tight, as though by his grip upon her he would give her an assurance of safety, he said:

"Take you with me, little one, of course I will. And now that is settled we will talk over our plans, for I think we ought to leave by that ten-thirty Western-bound service. Each hour after to-night, the service will become more crowded, and we had better avoid the crowd, if we can."

George Bullen had never had much to do with women. No woman had ever quickened by one extra beat his heart or pulse. Yet now he felt himself strangely, mysteriously drawn to this sweet young Lebanon girl. He realized that it was no time for love-making, yet he would have been of marble not to have been moved by her trust in him, and by her sweet, gracious personality.

At ten-thirty that night they were clear of the place, and homeward-bound to England.

CHAPTER XII.

ANTI-"WE-ISM."

SIR Archibald Carlyon, proprietor of the "Courier," and Ralph Bastin's employer, had just arrived at the "Courier" office. The whilom middle-aged, sprightly old man was as bowed and decrepit as a man of ninety.

As he entered the editorial private room, Ralph, for one instant, did not recognize him. Then, as he realized who it was, he sprang forward with an almost son-like solicitude, and helped him to a chair.

"Sir Archibald, what has happened?" he cried.

The old man lifted weary, hopeless eyes, out of which all the old-time flash had gone, and nothing but heavy dullness remained. "Have *you* heard from my boy, from George?" he asked.

"No, why, is there anything the matter, Sir Archibald?" Ralph's tones were full of alarmed anxiety.

The baronet's hand had been thrust into his breast-pocket, as he spoke. He took out a letter and handing it to Ralph, groaned out the two words:

"Read that!"

Ralph caught his breath as his eyes took in the first lines: "Dear Uncle, by the time you receive this, I shall be beyond *this* life, though *where*—in that outer world, that world beyond—I can—not tell."

Ralph had not turned to the signature, he knew the writing too well, and knew it for bright, happy jocund George Carlyon's. He read on:

"All that has happened in the world, of late, has driven me mad. Dear old Tom Hammond wrote me fully of his change of heart, and besought me to face the whole matter of my 'eternal destiny,' as he termed it. I simply did not reply to his letter. Three days later he was taken, with all those others, to God. Since then I have plunged into everything trying to drown thought, and remorse, but I cannot, so I am ending all—there's a mad thing to say, as if death could end all. Though I do not doubt but what many other fellows will do what I am doing now. Good bye, good old Hunky Archie,

"Your unhappy, rotten,

"GEORGE."

As Ralph lifted his eyes from the paper he found Sir Archibald's fixed upon him, and the anguish in the poor old dull eyes drew tears to Ralph's.

"We found him," cried the old man, "in the boat-house, by the lake, with a bullet through his temples. My poor boy! My noble boy!"

Dry-eyes, but with a soul full of anguish, his features, too, twisted with the anguish of his soul, the old man rocked himself for a moment in his chair.

Looking up suddenly, he startled Ralph by the bitterness of his tones, as he said:

"God forgive me! But I could find it easy to curse our clergy, our ministers, our bishops, our teachers, for that when we looked to them, and *paid* them, to tell us the right, the true thing, they let us go on deluded by the belief that attendance upon the *outward form* was sufficient to make us sure of Heaven in the future. Why, Bastin, good fellow, do you know that more than half of the clergymen with whom I was *well* acquainted, are among those whom God has left behind, and not one of those whom I know, thus left, has a mite of concern about their state, but seem to have gone right over to the Devil, if I may so say it. What does it all mean?"

Ralph began to speak kindly, sympathetically to him, but the old man suddenly interrupted with:

"And yesterday's article in 'the Courier' upon the opening of that Temple at Jerusalem, with all that about the 'Mark of the Beast;' that mock (I suppose it was *mock*) miracle, with the fire consuming the sacrifice, and then that awful portent of darkness, thunder, and lightning—but no rain. It reminded me of the scene at Calvary, when the Christ was crucified. What *does* it all mean, Bastin?"

"What I have said in that article, I believe, Sir Archibald. The events in Jerusalem, during the last three days are the beginning of the reign of Anti-christ. For years, blinded by Satan whom most of us, unknowingly, served, and blinded by what we termed the 'Progress of the Age,' and of the World, but which ought to have been recognized for what it really was, the growing of the Apostasy, which has now begun to be avowed and absolutely universal—blinded, I say, by all this, Sir Archibald, we suffered many mighty forces to stealthily, powerfully work together so that the climax that has come upon us, was made absolutely easy.

"If we had known our Bibles only a tithe as well as we knew our newspapers, we should have seen that all we were glorying in, under the name of 'Progress,' was but a perfecting of human systems, leaving God, and His purposes, and His plans utterly out of the question. We went to our churches, our chapels, we had a '*form* of Godliness,' but we tacitly, and controversally, in **print** and speech, 'denied the *power* thereof.' We not only made it possible, but easy 'for one man of Master-mind to assume universal dominion, and to be the object of universal worship, as Apleon, the Anti-christ, soon will be.'

"And now, Sir Archibald, we are on the eve of a gigantic blend of all religions, with all commercial undertakings. The more I study God's word in the light of all that is happening, the more clearly I see this.

"How often, in the old days—say from the mid-eighties—professing Christian men, when expostulated with as to the difference between their professed creed of the Sunday, and their daily practice in business, would say, 'oh, bosh! religion is one thing, business is another!' Then, as the years moved on, all kinds of trading concerns sprang up professedly religious, and conducted on professedly religious lines. But even the truest Seers in the Church of God would hardly have dared to predict that in a comparatively few years the final outcome of this trend in events would be an absolute coalescence into one vast system of the world's many religious systems and of the world's commerce. The most that the Seers of God, in His church, dared to say of the future was that the *principle* of such a *combined* system was suggested by the text of Rev. xiii. For the second Beast 'caused the earth and them that dwell therein to worship the first Beast . . . . And he had power . . . to cause that as many as would not worship the image of the Beast should be killed. And he causeth all, both small and great, rich and poor, free and bond, to receive a mark in their right hand, or in their foreheads, and *that no man might buy or sell, save he that had the mark, or the name of the beast, or the number of his*

name.' Here, for nearly two thousand years, was the
principle of this Hell-devised, Devil-developed combined
system of religion and commerce, prophesied, but now
few even of God's choicest saints realized all that would
mean.

"The nineteenth and early twentieth century Christendom had lost the Bible ideal of Christianity, and had
substituted a very material idea for God's idea. The two
decades—last of the nineteenth, and first of the twentieth
centuries—were marked by immense religious activities,
but while a merely religious movement might manufac-
ture a Christendom, it could never make Christians.

"To be religious is one thing to be a Christian quite
another thing. The vast bulk of the members of the
so-called Christian Churches of those years, had never
been born again from above.

"Christian in name (by virtue of membership in a
Church; or by virtue of their subscription to a creed; or
by a careful attendance upon the forms of their own
particular church) they were yet *only religious,* because
God's word regards those only as *Christians* in whom
Christ indwells, and none can be indwelt by Christ save
those into whom He has come in the birth from above.
('Born again' ones.) *'Except* a man be born again, he
CANNOT *see* the Kingdom of God' much more live in it.

" 'That which is born of the *flesh* is flesh,' and 'flesh
and blood cannot inherit the Kingdom of God,' but only
those *spiritually* born—born from above. We only
become Christians by *re*-generation.

"In the years immediately before the 'Rapture,'
professing Christians, and even *professedly* Christian
ministers, men who had taken vows before God to
preach the 'whole counsel of God,' and who received

their salary avowedly for this purpose, scouted, and often publicly denied the necessity of the New Birth. Blind leaders of the blind, they surely will have the greater punishment.

"But to return to the other thought.

"The last twenty years of the nineteenth century, and more so the first ten years of the twentieth century, was marked as an age of centralization and concentration of all kinds of interests, commercial, and religious. Each year, the trusts and monopolies in the commercial world became more and more concentrated, until it has become perfectly easy for Lucien Apleon, Emperor-Dictator of the World, to govern and control (from that beautiful, hellish city, Babylon the great,) every business interest in the world.

"Two days ago, at Jerusalem, the 'Covenant Sign'—so called—but which God calls the 'Mark of the Beast'—was donned by three or four million people, in the *holiday* spirit. But what was donned voluntarily, in a holiday spirit, forty-eight hours ago, will have to be *branded* on every one's person in the universe in three and a half years time—or less—or else the refuser of the degradation will have to seal his or her loyalty to God by their life.

"In three and a half years from now, Sir Archibald, the image of Lucien Apleon, will be set up in the Temple of Jerusalem, and, I believe, in every other great religious centre of the World——St. Peter's, Rome; St. Paul's, London; and so on in all our great cities, and world centres. I have been studying this subject naturally, and I find that one great scholar (Hengstenberg) says, that though *one* image is spoken of, yet having regard to the sense of the original, 'a multitude of images is meant.' "

"But *religiously,* Bastin, religiously?" cried the old man. "How did the condition of things in the end of the nineteenth, and the beginning of the twentieth centuries, help to make it possible for all the world presently to *worship* the Beast, and his image?"

There was an almost childish querulousness of tone in the old baronet's questioning.

"All those years," began Ralph, "were marked by a wonderful activity on new lines of deliverance for the human race, from the ills that had grown up around the vast bulk of that race. God's plan was for man's *regeneration,* a change of heart and life—a working from the centre to the circumference. But the churches —*all* denominations—of the years we are speaking about, began endless schemes of deliverance that the man, as they hoped, might be changed from the *out*side—that is to say, man's idea of benefitting man was by an *outward* reform.

"They failed to recognize the fundamental fact that all the 'Ills of Humanity,' so called, proceeded from man's natural depravity, from man *himself,* and not from his environment. We failed to see that a *reformed* race would only mean a perpetuation of all the old natural lusts, and presently, bring about a return to the old condition of things, while a *regenerated* race would hold reform in it, and that that reform would not only be perpetual, but ever increasing in its perfecting.

"Then, too, the great religious denominations became fired with the idea of a consolidating, unifying process that should smelt down all denominations into one. To do this every type of religion should find a place. What would it matter if one or more of the religions denied the Deity of Christ? that others did not accept the Bible as the Inspired word of God and so on? 'The doctrine of Christ,' was gradually eliminated from almost all preaching and the doctrine of a divine humanism—'The divinity of man,' became largely the new cult.

"I believe, from all that I can gather, one of the first steps towards this elimination of 'the doctrine of Christ,' could be traced in the continued elimination from the various denominational hymn-books (as *new* ones were issued beginning as far back as the late seventies) of hymns relating to the facts of the Atonement and other kindred subjects, and the substitution of odes, poems, etc., in which aspiration took the place of experimental religion. The hymn-books of more than one, or two, or three denominations, showed this retrograde movement, through their several successive issues.

"Then, side by side with this *Anti*-christian movement, there went on silently that gathering out from the world, and from the merely professing Christian church, those who were, by virtue of their New Birth, through faith in Christ, the recipients of Eternal life, and who, when that glorious 'Rapture' took place awhile ago, were caught up into the air as a *body* of living believers to be joined for ever, to their head—Christ; thus robbing the world of what Christ Himself called 'the salt of the earth.'"

With a groan, Sir Archibald cried:

"God help us, Bastin! What fools we were!"

Then with a weary upward look into Ralph's face, he rose to his feet, saying:

'I must be going. I've arranged to meet the lawyers in half-an-hour from now. Good-bye, dear fellow. I will come up to town to see you, or you must come down to see me, before the wind-up of the paper. Good-bye."

The two men wrung each other's hand, then parted.

Ten minutes later George Bullen and Rose arrived. Amazed to see his friend with an extraordinary beautiful girl, Ralph was presently listening to all the wonderful story of their meeting, etc.

Later on, when, for a moment or two, the two men were alone together, in the inner room, Ralph asked George what he proposed to do with the beautiful girl?

"There is but one thing I can do," he replied. "I must marry her, and that soon. It is no time, in the ordinary sense, to be thinking of 'marying and giving in marriage,' yet, under the circumstances, I can do no other. I care for her already, as I never cared for any woman, and her affection for me is touching in its clingingness."

He smiled a little sadly, as he added:

"It is well that there is a little company of us here in London, Believers in God, and therefore believers in marriage."

*   *   *   *   *

George Bullen and Rose were married within the week of their landing in England. The ceremony took place in a little company of believers, who gathered on Sunday (old-count of time) and once on a week-night, in a little hall that had been used for a Sunday School in the old days. Sunday Schools, like many of the other religious institutions, of the old days before the "Rapture," were quite a thing of the past.

Marriage was one of the things of the past. Some

years before the "Rapture," a booklet entitled "We—ism" had been published, in which the author had unblushingly declared: "Women, *absolved from shame,* servitude, and inequality, shall be enfranchised, owners of themselves * * * We believe in the sacredness of the family and the home, *the legitimacy of every child,* and the inalienable right of every woman to the absolute possession of herself."

The doctrines and practice of "affinity," the "problem" plays, and "sex" novels, of the first decade of the twentieth century, had all materially helped to make the unregenerate mind and heart ready to receive "free love" in its widest, grossest forms. While a certain teaching of "Christian Science" had had an overwhelming power in the same direction.*

All these forces had helped to make the doctrine of illicit love acceptable in these early days of the Antichrist reign, so that it was only among the little gatherings of true Believers, that marriage was sanctified into the sacrament it had been in the *good, true* old days.

---

*We prefer, in a book of this character, to keep back the actual terms of the filthy statement. Author.

CHAPTER XIII.

"THE ABOMINATION OF DESOLATION."

THE three-and-a-half years since the Covenant with Lucien Apleon, on the night before the opening of the Temple in Jerusalem, had been signed, had practically expired.

God's judgments had been seen in many ways upon the earth during these forty-two months. The position which Apleon now held, as the "World's Dictator," had not been the work of a day. Wars, no longer local, but practically universal had, for many long months at a time, been the order of the history of the world. "Nation shall rise against nation, and kingdom against kingdom."

These wars occupying only months at this period, would have occupied scores of **years** had they been events of the mid-nineteenth century. But with the perfection of hideousness—one might safely write *Hellishness*—of war's latest devices the work of destruction, and almost annihilation became short and sharp.

'Aerial warfare helped to bring about this consummation more speedily. The firing of a bomb or of a torpedo from an aerial war engine often accomplished in an hour what could not have been accomplished, a few years before, under months, often years of old-fashioned war.

These fearful conflicts were not confined to those of kingdom and nation against kingdom and nation, but citizens of one city fought with themselves, civil war was "on the rampage." The lust of war, the lust of blood, born of vile passions, burned in the breasts of men and women—for with the growth of the "woman's rights" question, and the establishment of the "equality of the sexes," bands of women fought bands of women.

These Amazons, indeed, wrought even fouler cruelties and butcheries than the men, for as there is no fouler odour under the sun than that of rotted lilies, so the depths to which "the lilies of the human kind"—women —will descend is fouler and deeper than the abysses of fall of men.

The hideous wars—international, civil, and *personal* conflicts—resulted, as wars ever do, in famine and pestilence. Only in this case, these later horrors had been fearfully aggravated, terribly prolonged.

The picture of the famine is most striking. The rider of the *black* horse is shown bearing a pair of scales, typifying the exactitude of weight—for single grains counted in these days. A man's full day's wage would purchase only a pint and a half of wheat (a chœnix) and that would form but a *scant* feeding for the day for himself. But there will then not be wheat enough to go round, and people will hail barley with the rapture of starving souls.

The tendency of the days in which we write these lines, is an ever-increasing luxury in eating and drinking, and this, too, among all classes.

That tendency will increase more and more, so that the inhabitants of the famine stricken earth will feel scarcity more than they would otherwise have done.

The pestilence followed the famine, until from war, famine, and pestilence a fourth of the entire population of the earth was swept away.

During the last twelve months quite a crop of false Christs had arisen. Each of these, in his turn, had had a certain following for a brief period, and each had had an untimely end.

The only really notable impostor was a man who had suddenly appeared in London, and who had immediately attracted immense attention. His knowledge of scripture, of the prophecies especially, was marvellous to those whom he addressd. No one ever attempted to verify his quotations, much less his connections of scriptures. For as Jannes and Jambres, Pharaoh's two chief Magicians, withstood Moses by demonology and jugglery, so, by a hellish jugglery, did "Conrad the Conqueror" (as this false Christ styled himself) juggle with the scriptures.

Apleon, the Anti-christ, had, apparently, taken no notice of any of the petty tribe of mushroom-like false Christs. That he was well acquainted with the sayings and doings of each of them goes without saying, as it was equally so as regarded this more presumptious of the crew "Conrad the Conqueror." There were many, in London especially, who wondered that Apleon did not appear and refute this man's claims, if they had no foundation.

The evident success of the imposter wrought his own downfall. Inflated with his success he publicly declared that Apleon would perish beneath a blast of his (Conrad's) nostrils, and announced that on a certain evening at ten o'clock on St. Paul's steps he would publicly re-state his claims, and also defy Apleon.

In the first year after the Rapture, the whole of the shops and warehouses on both sides of Ludgate hill, with all the purlieus at the back of each range of buildings, had been demolished, so that a huge open space, spreading fan shape, (the handle at St. Paul's) swept out, ever-widening, on the left as far as the approach of Blackfriar's Bridge, on the right through Farringdon Street to the Viaduct Bridge.

Within this space a million people could not only have congregated, but have heard distinctly, without any effort, the merest whisper spoken into the latest phone discovery the "Hearit." As, too, every bit of that open space was many yards below the level of St. Paul's steps, every one had a perfect view of all that transpired there.

The night in question, when the latest and greatest of the false Christs, "Conrad the Conqueror," had arranged to defy Apleon, proved to be exceptionally dark.

Three quarters of a million people were gathered in "The Fan"—that open space had been christened "The Fan" on account of its shape. It was admirably lit by the new light "Radiance," while a perfect blaze of radiance illumined the huge scarlet-covered, scarlet-draped platform that had been erected immediately in front of the steps of the Cathedral. (It was all very stagey, very theatrical, but then that was characteristic of the new age and regime.)

The false Christ appeared, and was greeted with a curious mixture of groans and hisses, and of cheers. (A keen judge might have been pardoned·if he had said that the bulk of the cheers were ironical.)

Speaking in his ordinary voice, the suction plates of the "Hearit" transmitted his words to the farthest remove of that "Fan" so that all could easily hear.

With a kind of gentle gravity, at first, he began by saying:

"Nearly nineteen hundred years ago when I walked this earth, at my first advent, I warned my disciples—

and through them the world—that many false Christs would come, but when it was said 'Lo, here!' or 'Lo, there!' that they were not to go hither and thither, many of these false Christs have appeared, and have tried to lead the people astray. Oh foolish people! How easily were they bewitched! And how worse than foolish the imposters were. They might have known that I should not have suffered them to take My Name in vain."

For ten minutes he talked thus, then suddenly changed his tone, and raising his right arm—it was long, thin, gaunt, and the wide-flowing sleeve of his white seamless robe, fell back showing the lean limb almost to the shoulder—he poured out a defiant speech against Apleon, adding "I have challenged! I wait for my challenge to be accepted."

A sudden, awesome silence fell upon all the gathered, listening thousands. They had not long to wait, for in that same instant a fierce crimson light shone in the dark heavens above them, and looking up they saw a fiery ruby scroll like flame rushing downwards through the sky.

An instant later the fiery scroll resolved itself into the characters of the "Covenant Sign" ("The Mark of the Beast.") With a swoop, like that of some crimson Albatross, the thing descended until it seemed almost to touch the platform where the challenger "Conrad" stood. Then, to the amaze and delight of the vast audience in "The Fan," out from convolutions of the central sign of the "Mark," Apleon stepped on to the platform.

His aerial chair (on this occasion made in the form of his own "number and sign") rose swiftly again and hovered mid-air.

The false Christ was as white of face as his robe. He

visibly cowered and shrank before the coming of the giant figure of the World's Dictator, as the latter strode in three long strides across the platform.

For one brief second, amid the hush and silence of the absolute awe that rested on the mighty audience, challenger and challenged stood facing each other. Then Apleon's voice was heard, as with a sweep of his hand he uttered the one word:

"PERISH, thou Fool!"

As his hand swept the air in the direction of the false Prophet, a wide sheet of flame leaped out of space, enveloped the white-robed figure, and it was instantly consumed. As at the burning of the sacrificial lamb at the dedication of the temple at Jerusalem, so now, the flame that had consumed the challenging imposter floated a yard or two over the spot where he had stood, and slowly resolved itself into "The Sign of the Covenant" ("Mark of the Beast,") in pure ruby flame.

"He doeth great wonders, so that he maketh fire come down from heaven on the earth in the sight of men, and deceiveth them that dwell on the earth by the means of those miracles which he had power to do."

Apleon turned towards the mighty gathering, and said triumphantly: "So perish all impostors!"

A thunder of cheers rose from three quarters of a million throats! Instantly followed by the chorus of the Apleon ode!

> "Hail! Hail! Hail Man of Men!
> World's Deliverer!
>
> APLEON!"

Like a living thing of writhing flames, the brilliant car swept downwards from the sky, where it had waited.

Almost, it seemed to skim the scarlet floor of the platform and to scoop up its owner, for none saw Apleon lift a foot to step into it, yet the next moment he was soaring away seated within the upper convolution of the serpent sign.

For hours, thousands of the people remained within the sweep of the great "Fan," talking of all that had occurred, and more absolutely convinced than ever that Apleon was God—*their* God.

Thrice during the next hour after Apleon's departure, three separate faithful souls—one of the three a woman—raised a testimony against the Man of Sin. But each one met with death within thirty seconds of their first utterance.

"And white robes were given unto everyone of them; and it was said unto them, that they should rest yet for a little season, until their fellow-servants also and their brethren, that should be killed as they were, should be fulfilled."

There were, scattered over all the earth, many thousands of believers in God, praying "Thy kingdom come." Many of these had turned to God during the first days of the shock of realization of "things as they truly were," when the "Church" had been translated to the heavenlies.

The number of these believers had been added to considerably, during the awful times of war, pestilence and famine, for these horrors (so plainly predicted in the word of God) had taught them to read their Bibles with new eyes, and to receive its truths and obey them. Of these believers, many had been, and many, many more were yet to be *"slain on account of the Word of*

God, and on account of the testimony which they held fast.

The whole of the three-and-a-half years had been rife with growing horrors, with licentiousness, and every evil possible to the unregenerate mind, and heart, and life, when full license is given to them.

The license and indulgence permitted—even arranged for, in the first instance—by the apostate church with a view to the more perfect enslavement of the world's worshippers, had brought forth a full harvest of evil. The effect of license is disorder, and presently anarchy. For three-years-and-a-half the apostate church had grown in assumption and in all abominations, and the effects of the license permitted, and *fearfully abused,* had produced a condition of things which became such an intolerable burden, that the time had become ripe for the *authority* in all this, to be destroyed.

The apostate church was the cause and the authority for all the excess of evil of the times, hence the ten-kingdomed confederacy which had at first buttressed the impious system, now, by united action, destroyed it. *"And the ten horns which thou sawest, and the Beast, these shall hate the harlot, and shall make her desolate and naked, and shall eat her flesh, and shall* BURN HER UTTERLY WITH FIRE. *For God did put in their hearts to do His mind,* AND TO COME TO ONE MIND, *and to give their Kingdom unto the Beast, until the words of God shall be accomplished."* (Rev. 17:16-17)

"Man is a religious animal!" And Lucien Apleon, endowed with special wisdom of his father and Master— the Devil—recognized this necessity for a religion from the outset of his career.

The Devil has always recognized religion, encouraged

it, and has even instigated it in a hundred forms, during the last 6,000 years. Only every effort of his Satanic power and force has been directed towards the luring of the religious soul *away from God*. The Devil is a Ritualist! He loves to entangle souls in a ritual, and the more sensuous the ritual, the better he is pleased, because such sensuousness and ritualism ministers to the "flesh," and while men and women's religion is fleshly, it cannot be spiritual. And the FATHER seeketh spiritual worshippers, "for they that worship Him, must worship Him in Spirit and in Truth." Then, too, Satan knows that all religiousness that is of the "flesh," tends to make its devotees anxious for the development of a good-self within them, while true, spiritual life *in Christ*, leads to the continual consciousness that *"in me, that is* IN MY FLESH, *dwelleth no good thing."*

Lucien Apleon encouraged religion, but not the religion of the Lord Jesus Christ—for he, Apleon was The *Anti-*Christ. It was he, with his emissaries, taught and guided by Satan, the Arch-enemy of God, and of His Christ, that had subtlety, secretly energized the world-religion, that followed the taking away of the church. That world-wide system had been an amalgamation of all the then existing false systems of religion. With the taking away of the church every type of license had been gradually permitted to the worshippers in the churches of this infernal system, until, at last, as we have seen, the governments had been compelled to abolish what at first they had helped to establish—for license had bred such a character and temper in the peoples that it became a menace to all order.

All this was part of Satan's organized plan, for, when the moment of the crushing out of this licentious, abominable religious system arrived, his plans, as regarded Lucien Apleon, The Anti-christ, were so perfected, by the ripeness of the world for the Anti-christ rule, that all else seemed plain sailing.

The poor, duped world knew Apleon only as the great SUPER-MAN, "long looked-for, come at last," the World's Deliverer, who was presently to be universally acclaimed as the World's Dictator.

The world had long been familiar with the system of private chaplains attached to great men's households. It was familiar knowledge to them that Dan, the Freebooter, (in the days of "The Judges") must needs have a renegade, runaway Levite for a priest, his salary thirty shillings a year, a suit of clothes and his victuals (as much as a renegade was worth). Absalom could do little, in his revolt, without the religious brand, so must needs have Ahithophel. And down to their own times, the World, at the period of Apleon's coming, was familiar with private chaplains.

Apleon's chaplain, a swarthy-skinned Jew (to all outward appearance,) was undoubtedly like Apleon himself, a Satanic resurrection, or if not a resurrection, certainly energized by the same infernal power. The Holy Ghost calls this man "The False Prophet." He exercised all the authority of Anti-christ, *"in his presence,"* as well as in his absence. *Eight* times the emphatic word *"he causeth"* is written of him, by the Holy Spirit, and a more hideous, lying, extraordinarily wicked catalogue of deeds is no where else to be found in the world's history:

"He causeth the earth, and *those that dwell in it,"* (does that refer to the foul spirits who dwell *in* that awful *under*-world, from which we believe the Anti-

Christ, as Judas re-incarnated came, or does it refer only
to dwellers on the earth? It may well mean *both!*)—
"To worship the first beast."

As well as his co-associate, Apleon—The Anti-christ,
the false Prophet not only claimed the power to work
miracles, but he *did* work them, showing a baleful but
powerful supernatural control over the forces of nature.
*"And he doeth great miracles . . . And he deceiveth those
that dwell* ON *the earth by reason of the signs which it
was given him to work in the presence of the Beast."* In
Egypt, three thousand four hundred or more years ago,
it was demonstrated by Jannes and Jambres that there is
a supernaturalism of the Devil, as well as of God,
against, as well as *for* God.

Both Anti-christ and his subaltern, the false
prophet, dealt largely in the miracle of fire. The *two
witnesses,* who had testified that they had come from
God, had consumed their persecutors, again and again
by fire, and the Hell-born imposters felt the necessity
of showing that they, too, could command fire.

Utterly destroyed by the ten kings, the world was
without an organized religion, and was ready for the
fouler, fuller rule of Satan—the worship of Anti-christ,
and his image.

As God had ever had a Trinity of personality and
power in Himself, so Satan in his damnable, deceivable
counterfeiting has now *his* trinity. Himself (Satan) the
embodiment of evil, the suggester, creator, energizer, he
makes a *mock* Christ—Apleon, the Anti-christ, answers
to the second Person of the divine Trinity. While
Apleon's chaplain, the false prophet, answers to the
third person of the divine Trinity.

Energized by Satan, even as Anti-christ himself is,

the false Prophet becomes a mighty force among the
world's peoples, persuading them that Apleon really is
God, and worthy of worship. The whole world has seen
and heard of the marvellous miracles of "The Prophet,"
as he is called.

The infatuation of all the world for the Man of Sin,
Lucien Apleon, was almost absolute and complete. He
ruled the world, every department of it—social, political,
commercial, religious. He blasphemed God. He blasphemed the translated Church that occupied the Heavenlies with her Lord.

Day by day, week by week, month by month he grew
bolder, more impious, more cruel, more persecuting to
the saints that were then living to God.

And through all this time Enoch and Elijah continued
their "witness" for their Lord. As judgment prophets,
they had been sent in this age of judgment, to resist the
awful, the gigantic blasphemies of Anti-christ, and to
give to the poor, vain, deluded world its last awful warning. For bad as had been the apostate Church, so
recently destroyed, the worship of Anti-christ himself,
would be infamously more impious.

The world hated them, yet *feared* the two witnesses.
More than once when blatant blasphemers, agents of
Apleon, had openly opposed them, and cursed them
and their witnessing, these witnesses of Jesus Christ,
"the faithful and true witness," had sent forth fire from
themselves and consumed their enemies. And the world
had learned to fear them, though they ignored their
warnings.

Many times, too, they had wrought fearful, havoc-
making miracles, so that as it was with the Egyptians
in the days of Moses, so it came to be with all the peoples

who witnessed the miracles of these prophets, Enoch and Elijah, for they shut the Heaven, in many places, "that rain should not fall during the days of their prophesying." They turned the waters into blood, and "smote the earth with every plague as often as they willed." Until the people hated, and *feared* them, yet, all the time, they hardened themselves against God, and the testimony of the two prophets, as Pharaoh hardened himself against God.

The multitudes learned that though they were absolutely powerless to hurt the TWO WITNESSES themselves, yet, given that THE WITNESSES were not present the mob found that they could work their will upon their followers—and they did, continually.

It was the morning before the great event that had been announced, the nature of the coming event was not known, though a hundred speculations were rife. The city was astir early, for the night had been too sultry for much sleeping, and everyone was more or less excited, as to *what* would be the great event which the next thirty hours—more or less—was to bring. As the sun mounted higher and higher the whole of the districts around the city belched forth their tens of thousands of curious people of every nationality, their goal the city itself.

Suddenly—the suddenness was like some magical effect—the two worst-hated beings in all the world, appeared on a mound of marble blocks, within a hundred yards of and *out*side the Jaffa Gate.

They were God's two gracious, faithful WITNESSES. The multitudes began to converge towards the spot where they had suddenly appeared. (It was a curious fact, however much people might hate the testimony of the TWO WITNESSES they seemed to have no power to pass on, when once the men of God began to preach.)

"Men and brethren of every clime," rang out the voice of Enoch. "Once again, in the name of Jehovah—Jesus, we lift our voices to warn you of the shortness of the time left unto you in which to repent, and to turn unto God.

"Turn ye, turn ye, for why will ye die? as die you certainly will under the breath of the Christ, when He presently shall come—for He shall 'slay with the breath of His mouth.'

"We preach not the gospel of the grace of God which, aforetime, before 'The Rapture,' was preached, that gospel which was good news of glad tidings to all sinners. That gospel told how He had lived on earth for over thirty-years—God inhabiting a human body, for God was in Christ reconciling the world unto Himself—it told how He died a death of shame and agony, a substitute for sinners, so that whosoever should believe on Him, should not perish, but have everlasting life. And as many as believed on Him gave He power to become the sons of God.

"It told of His coming again to receive all those sons of God, dead or living, unto Himself in the Heavenlies. Less than four years ago He came. Thousands who knew the truth, but had not accepted it, before He came, did so after the RAPTURE of the saints, and thousands of those have already sealed, and many more thousands will yet, seal their faith with their blood.

"The days of our testimony draws shorter now, we have few more opportunities of warning you, and of witnessing to our God. But here, once more, this morn-

ing, we preach unto you the gospel of the Kingdom. The
gospel of the coming Kingdom of Christ.

" 'For He shall reign whose right it is, and of His
kingdom of peace, and joy, and love there shall be no
end.' For nearly two thousand years men have prayed
'Thy kingdom come.' It is coming soon, but before He
begins His reign, He shall put down all enemies under
His feet. None will be able to hide from Him for His
eyes will be as a flame of fire.

"Those who will *now* seek Him, accept Him as their
king, whether He comes in their life-time, or whether
they lay down their lives as faithful witnesses to His
coming, all such we proclaim, shall live the glorious life
which He has for such."

The crowd numbered a hundred thousand now, and
the majority of them kept up a sullen murmur against
the preaching.

A native prince of a notable eastern realm, plucked a
javelin-type of weapon from his cumberband and hurled
it full into the face of the preacher. It never reached
its mark, but, boomerang like, it returned to the thrower
and shattered and entered his right temple.

But for the density of the crowd, the eastern would
have dropped to the earth like a stone—for he was
dead.

A way was made for a few to drag the body clear of
the mob, then, once clear, those who dragged it thence
returned to the crowd. "Without natural affection,"—
a trait of the Times—had degenerated into "without
common humanity."

For half-an-hour longer THE TWO WITNESSES
preached, warned, pleaded with the multitude. Then they

stepped from the pile of marble blocks, and passed quietly away.

As was customary after every such session of testimony, the crowd split up into many groups and discussed the whole situation.

On this occasion some five hundred men and women, mostly Jews, who had received the testimony,* were moving off in a body, when an unlooked for incident occurred.

Through all the witnessing of God's two prophets, there had stood among the listening crowd, a tall, swarthy-faced man, richly attired, a Jew by race, (that was evident from the marked Hebrew lines of his face). The expression of his face, during the *WITNESSING,* had alternated between mocking and rage. Now his eyes

---

*The Author, in common with every other public speaker, and writer, on these themes, has been so often asked the question, "What of my loved ones who are out of Christ, how will they fare when we are gone, and the Church is gone?" Let me say that the more I study the Scriptures of the times of which this volume speaks, the more I am convinced that of the many who are brought to accept Christ (in the Gospel of His coming to reign, "the Gospel of the Kingdom,") through the sudden translation of the Church, even though they be ill-taught, perhaps only half-hearted, they will, under the preaching of the TWO WITNESSES, be wholly brought into fellowship with Christ, and will, themselves in turn, become faithful witnesses to the TRUTH. There is nothing in Scripture to warrant the belief that the preaching of the TWO WITNESSES will be confined to Jerusalem, and it is surely reasonable to suppose that London, Edinburgh, New York, Chicago, Berlin, and all other chief cities, will hear their voices in witness and warning. They will doubtless have thousands of converts, Jew and Gentile alike, or where will the great multitude whom John saw, come from. But all those left behind when Christ comes, who may be won to Him afterwards, will not only miss the glories of *the Heavenlies* with Christ, but will suffer persecution, and many of them death at the hands of Anti-christ and his emissaries. (Author.)

followed the departing band of men and women who were loyal to the Gospel of the Kingdom.

With a scornful, devilish laugh, he pointed to the departing people, as he cried: "If we cannot kill the spawn that preaches, why not kill the hatched-out ones?"

The crowd was ripe for anything. With a roar, like unto Hell itself, they raced after the godly band and in a moment surrounded them, brandishing the long murderous knives of the east, and revolvers of the west.

The foul work of wiping out the whole band of faithful ones began. Every shot went home, every knife found a faithful heart. The twin lusts of hate and of religious fanaticism burned in the breasts of the mob. It was a carnival of cruelty and blood. Everyone wanted to see it. Other thousands hearing the sound of the shots, poured through the gates of the city. Everyone wanted a sight of the *entertainment*—for this the slaying was regarded, as, of old-time, Rome entertained herself by filling the eighty thousand seats of the great theatre, to see the Christians thrown to the lions.

There was not a coign of vantage to which the mob did not climb. They climbed upon the roofs, the balconies, held themselves perilously upon the sloping verandas, they stood upon window-sills, and hung from electric light pillars, and tram-line standards. They shouted, and sang, and urged upon the slayers to mutilate as well as kill "the carrion."

Then, suddenly, above all the din, and above even the crack of revolvers, the great song of Apleon, that foul ode of idolatrous laudation, set to most wonderful music, rang out from thousands of excited throats. The song was Hell-born, and hellishly sung.

When, a moment later the whole mob had trampled upon the slain believers—wantonly, heedlessly trod upon them,—in their passage towards the city, the swarthy Jew who had incited the crowd to their deed of blood, lit a cigarette, and crossed to where his aerial-chair waited him. He stepped into the upholstered seat, and turned his head to watch the mob, then with that evil laugh of his, he muttered: "Men are but sheep after all, and will follow any bell-wether!"

To his waiting driver, he said: "Esdraelon." The next moment the chair rose in the air, and like some wondrous bird soared away, northwards.

The swarthy Jew was Apleon's Chaplain, the false prophet.

Jerusalem was enormously crowded. Thousands upon thousands of people had come up from Babylon, as well as from every part of the world. The news had been flashed all over the earth, that some world-important event in connection with the Emperor-Dictator, would take place during this last week of the first three-and-a-half years of the "Great Covenant."

At the time of the offering of the Morning Lamb, just as the course of officiating priests were preparing for the slaughter of the lamb, Apleon's resident viceroy, entered the Temple enclosure, followed by a military detachment, and, accompanied by Apleon's chaplain, he whom God the Holy Ghost has called the false Prophet. The latter ordered the priest in charge of the "Course," to cease the offering, and to the amazed pro- test of the priest, he laughed scornfully, vouchsafing no other explanation than that it was his and the Emperor's command, that *all* Jewish worship-ritual should cease.

The priests could do no other than obey the command, enforced, as it was, by the presence of the Viceroy, *and the military force.*

The High-Priest lived a mile away from the Temple. One of the minor officials went off to apprise him of this strange new order.

As the man made his way down the marble road to the city level, he met a ponderous motor-driven trolley of great length—the thing was evidently bound for the Temple. Two hundred workmen followed behind the trolley, and the Temple-messenger noticed that on the trolley, lying beside the huge coffin-like packing-case that formed its chief burden, were a number of hoisting and hauling tackles, with a pile of handspikes, jacks, etc.

It was an hour before the messenger returned, the High-Priest accompanying him. By that time wonders —*infernal* wonders—had been wrought.

From the packing case there had been taken a gigantic image of Lucien Apleon, and it had been reared upon a plinth of dark green marble, upon the tessellated platform *within* the Temple.

The statue was of gold, and upon the green marble plinth was engraved: "I AM THAT I AM!"

In amazed, frightened horror, the High-Priest gazed for one moment upon the idolatrous abomination, then, as his blood boiled with a holy, righteous indignation, he thundered forth the words:

"Thou shalt have no other God before me.

"Thou shalt not make unto thee any graven image, ... Thou shalt not bow down thyself to them, nor serve them: for I the Lord thy God am a jealous God—."

"Take that foul, idolatrous thing hence!" he cried, with passionate warmth. His eyes were fixed upon Apleon's chaplain, (the false Prophet) whose mocking

smile, as he stood by the gang of workmen, angered him
beyond measure.

Not a man moved at the order of the High-Priest, and
he thundered forth his command again:

"Take that abomination down, and hence, or I will
call upon Jehovah to send His judgment fire down and
consume you all, and the idol as well."

With a blasphemous oath, the false Prophet, spat in
the forehead of the fulminating Priest, and hissed:

"Silence, fool, idiot, driveller!"

As the foul spittle touched the face of the Priest, he
fell prone upon his back on the pavement of the Temple.
A dead hush fell upon everyone present, for as they
gazed upon the face of the dead Priest they saw that the
whole forehead became filled with the "Mark of the
Beast."

The silence of this awesome hush was suddenly,
startlingly broken by a peal of mocking laughter. It
came from Lucien Apleon's deputy, the false Prophet.

Then, more startling still, the lips of the golden image
parted, and in deep, solemn tones the idol cried:

"So perish all who shall dare to oppose the Emperor
Lucien's will."

This was no trick. It was not a mechanical device
within the image. It was not a clever piece of ven-
triloquism. Of this we are assured—the image actually
spoke. God's word cannot lie, and John, under the
command of God, wrote it down: *"It was given the
false Prophet to give spirit to the image of the Beast,
that the image of the Beast should even speak."*

"To give SPIRIT *to the image!"* What does that mean?
Does it mean that life was given to it, temporarily? Who
shall say? Certainly it *spoke!"*

Unseen, unnoticed, at the very moment that the High-Priest fell, slain by the false Prophet, there had entered the Temple, Cohen, who had been High-Priest for the *first* year of this new Temple's history.

He slipped away as the image uttered its speech. He met many of the priests of other of the Courses, as they were approaching the Temple, also numbers of the devout Jews of the city and its suburbs, and many from other parts of the world, who had been specially drawn hither by the news that had been flashed world-wide, as to some great event about to happen in Jerusalem.

"Stay!" he cried. His looks told of something serious, and in an instant he was the centre of an eager, anxious, enquiring crowd of Jews.

"Jehovah help us!" he went on. "For those who would be true to Him now, must be prepared for flight or for death. Apleon, is a traitor! *'He hath put forth his hands against such as be at peace with him; he hath broken his covenant.'* Psalm lv. 20. *'He confirmed a covenant with us for seven years.'* Daniel ix. 27. *'The words of his mouth were smoother than butter, but war was in his heart: his words were softer than oil, yet were drawn swords.'* Psalm lv. 21."

Cohen, even while he had been speaking had led the crowding Jews away from that main road, and now, in a *cul-de-sac,* he was continuing his words.

"Blind! Blind! that we were, all of us, I, especially, for my Gentile friend, the editor of 'The Courier'—London daily paper—warned me. He told me of the meaning of our own prophet Daniel's words, *'In the midst of the week* (the seven years of the covenant we made with that apostate) *he shall cause the sacrifice and the oblation to cease.'*

"This he has done this morning. The priests were stopped in their preparations for the morning sacrifice.

" '*And,*' said our father, Daniel, '*for the over-spreading of abominations he shall make it desolate, even until the consummation.*' Daniel ix. 27.

"Brethren, of the House of Israel, the Lord our God is one God. I am no Mehushmad, but in common with many of our rabbis, I have read the Gentile New Testament, and there, in the words of the Nazarene Prophet, (Matt. xxiv. 15, 16.) He prophesied exactly what has come to pass this morning in our beautiful Temple, for he said:

" '*When ye* (that is we of the House of Israel) *therefore, shall see the abomination of desolation, spoken of by Daniel the prophet, stand in the holy place* (of the Temple)—*whoso readeth, let him understand:—then let them which be in Judaea flee into the mountains . . . and pray ye that your flight be not on the sabbath day. For then shall be great tribulation, such as was not since the beginning of the world to this time, nor ever shall be.*'

"Jehovah help us, brethren! This morning has convinced me that these times are upon us. What *this* day will bring none but Jehovah can tell! My last word to you, my advice to you all, is, flee this city, flee the neighbourhood. For weeks I have had it borne in upon my soul, that the man we have covenanted with, was working some deep, subtle, hellish scheme. Now he hath shown his hand, there are but three courses open to us, *idolatry*—worshipping that idol set up in our holy place, yonder; *flight;* or *death.*"

Even as Cohen harangued his crowd of priests and Jews, Apleon rode up the white marble road to the Temple. The Hebrew crowd was quite hidden from any observation from that main road. It was well for them, doubtless, that it was so.

A moment or two after Apleon and the mighty throng which followed him had passed, the crowd of Jews left the *cul-de-sac,* and silently, anxiously dispersed in various directions.

Cohen found himself walking with the man who had been Hight-priest last year. Together they conversed in low, serious, guarded tones, until they suddenly discovered themselves close up to a mighty throng gathered about the now well-known witnesses, Enoch and Elijah.

The two priests paused to listen to the witnesses' denunciations of Apleon, whom they designated "The Beast,"—"The Anti-christ." Both men had listened often before to these prophets of God, and both had often been well-nigh convinced of the truth of the testimony of the two witnesses.

"It is said," whispered Cohen, to his fellow-priest, "that these two men are the two prophets of the Most High God, Enoch and Elijah—those two of God's servants who never passed through death."

"The three and a half years of their witnessing," replied the second priest, "have been crowded with incident, miracle, and much that has been supernatural. They say that no man has seen them eat. That, like Elijah, when upon earth, they too have been supernaturally fed. Then, too, nothing has been able to harm them. Apleon (the priest's voice was lowered to the merest whisper) has directed his agents to war against them over and over again. They have shot at them, hurled vitrol upon them, and tried to seize them, to bind them, but as they have themselves testified again and again, nothing can harm them *until they have finished their testimony."*

Cohen bent closer to his fellow-priest, as he whispered: "The book of Revelation, in the Gentile New Testament, declares that *'they shall prophesy a thousand two hundred and sixty days, clothed in sack-cloth. And when they have completed their testimony, the Beast that cometh up out of the abyss* (I believe that is Apleon) *shall make war with them, and overcome them, and kill them.'"*

"Now if this come to pass, then they will die to-day, for it is a thousand two hundred and sixty days, this very evening, since they began their preaching, and——. But, listen, to what the one of them is saying."

The voice of Enoch rang out as it had done five thousand years before, when he had prophesied, saying, *"Behold! the Lord cometh with ten thousands of His saints to execute judgment upon all; and to convince all that are ungodly among them of all their ungodly deeds which they have ungodly committed, and of all their hard speeches which ungodly sinners have spoken against Him——."*

But now the message of the prophet had in it testimony as well as warning:

"Have we not warned you for three years and a half, that the man, Apleon, whom you have all trusted in, was but the tool of his father, the Devil? Have we not told you often that he worked upon your deluded minds and imaginations for one purpose only, to keep you from 'The God of Salvation,' and that, presently, he would set up his own image to be worshipped in that gilded thing of unbelief, upon that mount, yonder?"

A peal of derisive, mocking laughter greeted this statement.

The voice of the prophet cut the laughter, with its supernatural incisiveness, so that it rose clear and distinct above the laughter:

"And now all that we prophesied has come to pass. The image of Apleon (the abomination of desolation) spoken of by Daniel the prophet, has this morning been set up in the Temple over there. *'And that Man of Sin .... opposeth and exalteth himself above all that is called God, or that is worshipped; so that he, as God, sitteth in the Temple of God, showing himself that he is God.'* 2 Thess. ii. 4.

"Upon the pedestal of his image, that was reared this morning, he has caused to be engraved the very name of our Jehovah God—'I AM THAT I AM!' as he supposes it to be, because it is thus translated in the Bibles of the world. There is no sense in that way of putting it, as there is no sense, nothing but vanity and coming failure and fall, in that 'Man of Sin' himself. But he has chosen to ape Jehovah-God by using *'I am, that I am!'* instead of the true translation which has evidently been hidden from him and which is: 'I AM HE WHO AM FOR EVER!'"

"He is Anti-christ, that denieth the Father and the Son. 1 John ii. 22. The Scriptures have been issued by millions, every soul of you here has had an opportunity of knowing the things whereof we again testify. You have heard, or read, or both, (or you could have done if you would) that he, the Man of Sin, *'would cause an image of himself to be made, that he would give life to it, and that the image should speak'* (Rev. xiii. 14, 15). All this has happened this morning, and all else will happen that is prophesied. Therefore we cry:

'Turn ye, turn ye, for why will ye die? Why should

ye be stricken any more? Ye will revolt more and more.
From the sole of the foot even unto the head there is no
soundness in you, but wounds and bruises and putrefying
sores: Wash you, make you clean; put away the evil of
your doings from before God's eyes; cease to do evil,
Turn ye, turn ye, for why will ye die?"

Strangely affected by the power and earnestness of
this witness of God, Cohen and his fellow-priest turned
reluctantly away. In the heart of each of them was the
determination to be clear of the Jerusalem neighbourhood that very forenoon, if possible. In fact before one
o'clock had struck, that mid-day, there had taken place
a really remarkable exodus from the city and its neighbourhood. Of these, many were Jews, in whose composition there was deeply engraved a deep-seated antagonism
to all idolatry.

Then, too, there were many "Kingdom believers" (by
what other name can we call them, since, having missed
Salvation by the "Gospel of Grace," they now served
God, while waiting for Christ's coming to set up His
kingdom.) Many of these fled the city and its neighbourhood, for they counted not their lives dear when it
came to a case of blasphemy and idolatry. Yet, because
the love of life is inherent with the race, and because,
too, these "Kingdom believers," learned to bring others
to God, before the final judgments came, and knowing
that it was written "that as many as will not worship the
image of the Beast shall be killed," they fled Jerusalem.

CHAPTER XIV.

DEATH OF THE "TWO WITNESSES."

A PLEON had been on the Temple mount for two hours. Part of that time he had been in the Temple itself, in and out of which there passed continually, streams of people, all curious to see the wonderful image of Apleon, the image that had spoken, and that had slain "unbelievers."

Apleon had watched the ever-moving crowds of dupes, and noticed how every one of them bowed, or prostrated themselves before his image. He noticed, too, whenever his own presence had been realized, that the worshippers, while bowing *before* the image faced him, Apleon, so that they really gave *him* the worship.

In spite of all that Romanists, and others of a similar cult, may say, the *worship* of an image or of a statue, means the worship of the person imaged or sculptured— this is the very essence of all image-worship. The great Chrysostom, in one of his records of his time, says:

"When the images of the Emperor are sent down and brought into a city, its rulers and multitude go out to meet them with carefulness and reverence, not honouring the tablet or the representation moulded in wax, but the standing of the Emperor."

Athanasius wrote:

"He who worshippeth the image, in it worshippeth the emperor; for the image is his form and likeness."

And the worship, in the Jerusalem Temple, of the

image of Apleon, ("The Beast") was the worship of the man himself.

There is a very curious word in Habakkuk ii. 9, *"Woe to him that saith to the wood, 'Awake!' to the dumb stone, "Arise, it shall teach."* Apleon, the Antichrist actually qualifies hmiself for that "woe" of God's.

A notice had been promulgated that in the "Broadway"—the wide, open square from which the great marble road to the Temple opened out,— throughout the whole day, the new "Covenant" brands would be affixed.

The "Covenant" sign, had for three years and a half been *mostly* worn (as we have seen) in the form of a ring on the right hand, or as a pendant frontlet upon the forehead. Some few million enthusiasts, it is true, had worn it *branded* on the flesh of the forehead, but this had not been universal.

Now it had been decreed by Apleon, and endorsed by his second, the false Prophet, that the wearing of a *detatchable* "Sign," be no longer permissable, that *all must be branded—or die.*

Brands, in several sizes, had been prepared, which, when pressed against the forehead, and worked by a spring-lever, left the damnable mark upon the skin in deep, rich purple characters. The surface of the branding instrument was peculiarly soft and yielding, so that when, by the automatic inking, the mark was made, there was never an imperfect sign, but every character was truly formed. The ink used, claimed to be absolutely indelible, and those who had tried it, more than two years before, had found no break in any single line or curve of either of the characters.

For two hours, a hundred branders had been at work

at their truly hellish task, and if the *donning* of the
badges, three and a half years before had been in a
veritable *holiday* spirit, the acceptance of the brand,
now, was with a blend of rapturous joy, and of actual
worship.

With the infernal cunning which has ever characterized Satan's efforts to thwart God and His Christ, he
has counterfeited every rite, every sacrament of Christ's
Church. Hence Apleon, Satan's tool, is very keen upon
this matter of a baptismal sign. He makes a sacrament
of it (i. e. an oath or covenant of fidelity.) To show
their allegiance to his infernal lordship, Anti-christ's
subjects must now wear his brand so that it can never be
erased or removed, and his chaplain ("The False
Prophet") *"causeth all, the small and the great, and the
rich and the poor, and the free and the bond, to receive"*
—literal translation—*"a stamp or brand, on their right
hand, or on their forehead."*

The preaching of the cross, of Jesus Christ as the
World's Redeemer, the putting away of sin, and the gift
of eternal life by faith in God's word of grace, the
baptism into the name of Christ, had, for several
decades, been growingly scouted as "foolishness." "An
obsolete doctrine," all that was voted. "Men are far too
intelligent to be bound by such a Bible creed as that.
New times need new doctrines," etc., etc.

The twenty years immediately preceding the manifestation of the "Man of Sin," had been characterized
by such utterances, and many others infinitely more
impious, blasphemous, and *senseless*. *"But after the
world by its wisdom knew not God, it was God's good
pleasure through the foolishness of the thing preached,
to save them that believe* . . . . Because THE FOOLISHNESS

OF GOD IS WISER THAN MEN." But when Anti-christ shall promulgate his devil-doctrines, senseless, idolatrous, humiliating, the bulk of men of every grade and class, will suffer themselves to be branded like cattle in a round-up. Believing "the lie," deluded by that universal lie, they will have no choice, save to be branded, or to die. And to yield themselves to the infernal brand will mean to be cut off for ever from God.

"*If any man worship the Beast and his image, and receive his mark in his forehead, or in his hand, the same shall drink of the wine of the wrath of God, which is poured out without mixture into the cup of His indignation; and he shall be tormented with fire and brimstone in the presence of the holy angels, and in the presence of the Lamb; and the smoke of their torment ascendeth up for ever and ever; and they have no rest day or night, who worship the Beast and his image,* AND WHOSOEVER RECEIVETH THE MARK OF HIS NAME.*" (Rev. xiv. 9-11.)

Simultaneous with the beginning of the branding, the two witnesses had taken up a position close by the branders, and had persistently witnessed to the near coming of the Lord in judgment upon those who wore the Mark of the Beast, while, at the same time, they denounced Apleon as the Anti-christ.

Over and over again during their testimony, attempts had been made to silence them, every conceivable death-attack had been made upon them—but nothing harmed them. No weapon formed against them could prosper. until their "witness" was completed. And every one who had assisted in any form, in attacking them, had died in the act.

Now, Apleon, attended by the ten kings, who had been summoned to Jerusalem, rode down from the

Temple. At the branding station, the ten kings dismounted, and each received the foul mark on the forehead.

As the last of them received the brand, a startled wondering cry burst from some of the multitude who thronged "The Broadway," and following the many pointing fingers of the startled ones, every one saw how that purple, lambent flames played about Apleon's forehead in the form of the "Covenant" sign.

"He doeth great wonders in the sight of men, and deceiveth them that dwell on the earth by means of these miracles." Rev. xiii. 12, 14.

"Power was given him over all kindreds, and tongues, and nations." Rev. xiii. 7. *"He shall do according to his will; and he shall exalt himself, and magnify himself above every God."*

Acclaiming him as very God, the people suddenly prostrated themselves in worship before the great deceiver.

Suddenly the voices of the two witnesses were heard. Both voices were clear and distinct, yet neither clashed with the other, even though each voice used separate terms. They stood about a hundred yards apart from each other.

Everyone rose to their feet, every eye was fixed upon the two grand, fearless faces, as they thundered forth their words of warning of judgment, of entreaty. Then suddenly they turned their gaze and their speech upon Apleon himself.

As the "Te Deum" sprang spontaneously from the lips of Ambrose and Augustine, each saint voicing an alternate stanza, so now the two witnesss hurled their fulminations against the Man of Sin:

"Thou heart of all foulness and deceiveableness, with the breath of His lips shall the Christ slay thee." Isa. xi. 4.

"Thou marked one, the Lord shall consume thee with the spirit of His mouth, and shall destroy thee with the brightness of His coming." 2 Thess. ii. 8.

"O thou enemy! Thy destructions shall soon come to a perpetual end." Ps. lx. 6.

"It shall come to pass in that day (when Jehovah shall deliver His people out of thy hands) *saith the Lord of Hosts, that I will break thy yoke* (Apleon Emperor, Man of Sin, Anti-christ) *from off the 'peoples' neck."* Jer. xxx 8.

"Judgment shall sit, and Christ shall take away thy kingdom, to consume and to destroy it unto the end." Dan. vii. 26.

"Tophet is ordained of old, yea for thee, thou Man of Sin, it is prepared: God hath made it deep, and large; the pile thereof is fire and much wood: the breath of the Lord, like a stream of brimstone, doth kindle it." Isa. xxx. 33.

"And thou shalt be taken, and with thee The False Prophet, thy co-adjutor, he whom thou hast deputed to work miracles before thee, and in thy foul name, and with all those whom thou and thy False Prophet have deceived, who have received thy brand on them, and who have worshipped thine image.—These all, you, your prophet, and your dupes, shall be cast into a lake of fire burning with brimstone. Rev. xiii. 2, 3. Rev. xix. 20.

Low and mocking, a laugh broke from Apleon, upon whose brow there still played that lambent flame. The laugh was caught up by the multitude, until one far-reaching volume of mocking, derisive laughter went rolling out-and-away from The Broadway, to Gareth and Goab, and every other suburb of the city, and back again.

As the last echo of the laughter died away, Apleon called, to his Viceroy:

"Where is the axe and the block?"

"Here, Sire!"

A score of men bearing broad, gleaming axes, with thrice a score of others, bearing, each three, a blood-red enamelled block, came forward into the centre of the square.

"Take those two drivelling prophets, and behead them!" cried Apleon.

A thousand hands were stretched towards the witnesses. This time they were readily taken. Their bodies were dragged to the blocks, and with one stroke to each, they were beheaded.

With a shout of triumph, that spread far and wide, the people acclaimed Apleon as "God Almighty."

"Let no man touch that carrion, to bury it!"

Was the order of Apleon.

That was to be doubly his hour of triumph. All arrangements had been made for his official coronation. An immense awning of purple and gold silk, was stretched over the whole of "The Broadway."

The time occupied in stretching the whole thing was not more than sixty seconds. A throne of Ivory, Pearl, and gold was set in the centre of the pavement, beneath the awning. Everything was done with the rapidity of a stage-setting in a theatre—*it was all very theatrical!*

A score of trumpeters executed a wonderful fanfare, then, amid more pomp than the world had ever yet seen, a crown, of fabulous value and of extraordinary magnificence, was set upon the head of Apleon, who occupied the throne, each of the ten kings actually touching, and helping to set the crown upon his head.

Hitherto, Apleon, though upheld by the ten kings and governments, had, after all, been an *un*-crowned Dictator. Now, in the hour of his seeming triumph over "The Two Witnesses," he was crowned Roman Emperor of the ten-kingdomed confederacy.

When the coronation ceremony was finally completed, and Apleon, mounted on his black horse, and surrounded by the ten kings, started to ride back to the Palace, he ordered messages to be flashed to all the cities of the world, announcing three days of rejoicing over the slaying of the Witnesses, and also the announcement of his own coronation.

The rejoicings in Jerusalem, Babylon, and elsewhere, over the death of "The Witnesses" was wilder than the "Mafficking" in England of the Boer war days. The two Witnesses had been a source of torment and fear upon all peoples (save those who clove to God) and now that their headless bodies lay stark and dead on the marble pave of "The Broadway," the people *"rejoiced upon them, made merry, and sent gifts one to another."* Rev. xi. 10.

The outrage upon decency, sanitation, and even common humanity, in suffering the two bodies to remain unburied, lasted three days and a half. Three days and a half was long enough period for the representatives of every nation, gathered in the city and neighbourhood, to be perfectly assured that they were dead. *"And certain ones from among the peoples and the tribes and tongues and nations behold their corpses three days and a half, and suffer not their corpses to be put in sepulchre."* Rev. xi. 9.

When Edward the 7th of Britain, lay dead in the great Abbey of the Empire, it was counted high honour to be part of the *silent* guard over the coffin.

And men almost fought for the privilege to stand guard over the headless forms of the Two Witnesses lying on that marble pave in Jerusalem: *"It cannot be that a prophet perish out of Jerusalem."* Luke xiii. 33.

But *these* death-guards were not silent. They laugh scornfully, derisively, and crack jokes upon the now silenced testimony of the Two Witnesses. Caricatures, and comic cuts upon their lives, their death, their oft-repeated warnings, were printed and sold in the streets of the city.

It was the evening of the fourth day after the setting up of the image in the Temple, and three and a half days since the Witnesses were slain. A last, a final public function before the dispersal of the kings, and others specially gathered for the coronation, and other ceremonies, had been arranged for 6 o'clock in "The Broadway."

Apleon, and the other kings had gathered. The trumpeters had blown one blast upon their silver instruments, when a cry of horror burst from the gathered multitudes. For the bodies of the Two Witnesses suddenly stood upon their feet.

They were facing Apleon, as they stood up. Their eyes met his startled, fearsome gaze. His face was deathly pale. A tomb-like hush of awe and fear was upon the gathered peoples.

Suddenly, overhead, *three* deep notes, like thunder rolled through space. The multitude thought it was thunder, the resurrected Witnesses knew it for the voice of their Lord, crying *"Come up hither!"*

And instantly their bodies rose in the sight of all the people. No awning was spread over the square, this evening, and every eye beheld the ascent of the resurrected saints, a wondrous cloud seeming to upbear them upon its billowy whiteness.

An overwhelming fear fell upon everyone. The arranged kingly function was suspended. Yet still the people remained. It was as though they were spellbound.

And while everyone waited, wondering and fearing, a low, deep rumbling was heard beneath their feet. Then the earth trembled, and rocked.

For one long, shuddering instant every voice was hushed, horror got hold of the people. Then in a moment yells and shrieks of terror escaped men and women alike. From the roofs of the houses there came piteous cries for help, for, with the trembling of the earth, the houses rocked like children's houses of cards.

It grew dark, and bewildered by the sudden awfulness of the whole situation, and maddened by the hopelessness born of the sense of insecurity of even the foot of ground upon which each stood, the mob rushed blindly hither and thither. Panic, in its most hideous form got hold of them. In their blind, unseeing rushes they collided with each other, and a score of fierce passions leaped to life within them, chief of which was a lust for war. Madly, savagely, senselessly, neither knowing or caring with whom they fought, they stabbed and shot, and clawed and scratched, and boxed and wrestled with each other.

The many horses stampeded, and beat down hundreds of the people beneath their iron hoofs.

The darkness deepened, it grew sooty, inky. The

horrors pressed upon the people, women and children, and even men grovelled on their faces in the dust, clutching and clawing at the ground.

Thunder in the heavens, and thunder under the earth deafened and terrified every soul. Fierce, wide, jagged ribbons of awful flame came out of the blackened heavens. Scores of thunderbolts, red and flaming, leaped out of the blackness of cloud above, and, hissing as they came, wrought awful death among the mobs upon which they descended. The smell of burning flesh filled the air, making a new horror.

The thunder and rumble beneath the earth increased. The whole surface of the city heaved like the swell of a storm-tossed sea. Chasms, fissures, gulfs yawned every-where, and thousands of people toppled into the opened earth. Suddenly, the whole heavens were filled with an appalling succession of frightful crashings; it was as though hundreds of millions of powerful rockets were exploding in successive volleys of millions each. Beneath the earth, thunders and crashings went on at the same time. Then, in every direction, the earth fissured and gaped and yawned wider than ever, and with blood-curdling roarings and crashings, a whole tenth part of the city tottered and fell into the yawning gulfs, with thousands upon thousands of people.

Slowly, the rumble of falling buildings, and the hideous thunders below and aloft died away, and a strange, awesome hush fell upon the city. Slowly, too, the darkness melted, leaving the sky blood-red. The blood gradually merged into pink towards the centre of the dome, the pink became gold, then every living eye in the city and suburbs became centred upon that golden centre, and all saw the forms of the Two WITNESSES, with a pavement of dazzling white cumulus beneath their sandalled feet.

The wondrous scene was as the very voice of God to the watching multitudes, if they could but have understood, the voice testifying to the power and truth of God and His word.

It was the *new,* the fashionable part of the city that had suffered in the earthquake and its attendant horrors—the part of the city where "Satan's seat was," chiefly.

With the engulphing of the most fashionable part of the city, there was a consequent heavy toll of human life. Seven thousand men of name, of notable rank, perished in the earthquake.

When the last building had tottered into the yawning chasms of the riven earth, and the souls of the late deriders of God had toppled into their hell; when the clouds of dust had cleared away; when no further earth-rumble came, then with a gasp of terror the remainder of the gathered thousands of people *"Gave glory to God."*

There was no worship; no sorrow for their sin; no repentance; not even any remorse; certainly no conversions of the whole mass, any more than were of Jaunes and Jambres, when they declared, of the Miracles of Moses and Aaron, *"This is the finger of God."*

Some there were, who had been near to yielding to the pleadings of the Two Witnesses, who were wholly won to God in this hour, but the vast mass of the people continued to worship the Beast. Their cry to God had been but a terror-stricken cry.

By the morning the gathered masses had wholly recovered themselves, and the suspended public function was carried out. One part of this function was the partition of Palestine among certain rulers, millionaires, and others. *"He* (Anti-christ) *shall divide the land for gain."* Dan. xi. 39.

With the horror and fear of the survivors of this earthquake, the *"Second Woe"* was finished, *"and behold the third woe cometh quickly."*

CHAPTER XV

FLIGHT! PURSUIT!

THROUGHOUT the latter half of the "Day of Blasphemy," when the "Abomination of Desolation," had been set up in the Temple of Jerusalem, the exodus of fearsome, fleeing people went on. With nearly three million visitors, from every land, the more or less rapid departure of a hundred thousand or more, was not noticed. In fact, more than that number of persons might be expected to leave every twenty-four hours—the ordinary exit of visitors after the special visit.

But, presently, it was reported to Apleon, that a mighty exodus of Jews and Gentiles, few of whom wore the "Brand of the Covenant," had taken place, and was still taking place. He had spies everywhere.

The whole of Jewish population, with those on visit to the city for this special occasion, were either *for* the Anti-christ or *against* him, those against him were but a very small minority.

The deluded, idolatrous Jews will hate and betray their nearest and dearest relations and friends, as Micah prophesied that they would : *"Trust ye not in a friend, put ye not confidence in a guide; keep the doors of thy mouth from her that lieth in thy bosom.* Micah vii. 5. And endorsing this, Jesus said : *"They shall deliver you up to be afflicted, and shall kill you: and ye shall be hated of all, for my name's sake. And then shall many be offended, and shall betray one another, and shall hate one another.* Matt. xxiv.

With father, mother, brother, lover, sister, friend all acting as betrayers of their own kith and kin, Apleon soon learned much that he needed to know as to the fugitives. He discovered that the many thousand fleeing Jews had, first, at least, travelled southwards, and he instructed his emissaries to ascertain the objective point of these fleeing Jews. He left the whole thing in the hands of his chaplain, "The False Prophet," who had the essence of all the subtlety of Hell in his composition, with all the devilish ingeniousness of cruelty of every Inquisitor who had ever practised in past days. A "lamb" in seeming, he was a "dragon in actual nature." Rev. xiii. 11.

Spies had informed him that Cohen, the first high-priest, was undoubtedly the leader of the fugitives, but that his wife and daughter had refused to accompany him. "They are wholly with our World-Lord, Apleon," one of the spies had said.

"Will Cohen, think you," asked the chaplain, "steal back under cover of one of the dark nights and try to induce his wife to join him?"

"No," laughed the spy. "He will think himself well rid of her. She has been the plague of his life. Every drop of her blood is as sharp as the juice of a lime. Her lips distil wormwood. And vinegar is a cloying sweetness compared to her kindest thought or utterance, and ——"

"But the daughter," interrupted the chaplain, sharply, "What of her? Is she a replica of her mother?"

"Not a bit, not a bit of it!" And the eyes of the betrayer flashed with a new light. "Miriam is as beautiful as a houri, as fair as the light of a sun-lit day after a black night of tempest, and as sweet in disposition as Rachel, the favoured of our father Jacob."

"If she is all this, why is she unwed? or perhaps she loves, and perhaps we could make her a tool of her lover, and thus find out where her father has led those dogs of fugitives."

There was a look of hate and malice in the eyes of the betrayer, as he answered: "Yes, she loves, loves as her very life, but the man she loves is an even greater zealot than her father, and he has gone with Cohen—curse him! may he never more be seen by Miriam!"

The chaplain laughed maliciously: "Oh! the wind blows in that quarter, eh? You love the fair Miriam, but another has cut you out!"

The betrayer was inclined to be surly, but the chaplain knew how to speak like the *"lamb,"* and quickly mollified the young Hebrew. Then, together, they plotted and conferred, their plotting based on the supposition that young Isaac Wolferstein, the fugitive lover of Miriam would return, secretly, to induce Miriam to share the loyal-to-Jehovah flight of himself and her father.

* * * * *

The vineyard of Cohen was an eighth of a mile from his villa, and the villa was a mile and a half from the Jaffa Gate of the city. Miriam had wandered out as far as the vineyard, for her heart was too sore to sleep that night. She made her way to the arbour, where so often Isaac and she had held sweet and tender intercourse. During the last twelve hours, she had turned unto God and unto the Messiah who was so soon to come to deliver His people and to set up His kingdom.

She had gazed upon the resurrected Two Witnesses, as they had appeared, glorified, in the Heavens, after that awful earthquake. And, recalling the words of their preaching, and all that her lover and father had urged upon her before they reluctantly left her, to flee the city, she had been suddenly bowed before God, in penitence and prayer.

"If only Isaac would come back for me," she moaned, as she dropped wearily upon the seat of the arbour.

"He has come back, Mirry, darling!"

At the first sound of the voice that spoke, she leaped to her feet, crying: "Isaac! Isaac! Forgive me, dear, that I——"

She got no further, his arms enclosed her fair form, his hot lips gave and received love's pure caress, and when at last he spoke again, it was to say: "God has given us again each other, darling, and nothing but death must ever part us again."

The hours passed and to them they seemed but as minutes. He had much to tell of the flight of the Believers, as he termed them, and had many words of message from her father.

The morning comes early in Palestine. At the first blush of dawn they stole out of the vineyard, to where his motor waited. They had eyes only for each other, as, hand in hand, they moved through the morning twilight. Then, with a bewildering suddenness, from the off-side of the motor, a dozen crouching men sprang out.

Five minutes later, amid the mocking, jeering laughter of their captors, they were being taken to the city—only not together. Miriam was forced to ride *in* the car seated by the side of their betrayer, the man whom she hated, and whose love-overtures she had scorned and repulsed.

Her wrists and her ankles were bound with cords, and she had been lifted into the car, bodily, by the man of her hate. To humble her and to shame her, the cur had kissed her again and again before her captive lover, then with a carefully judged malice, he had seated her, by his side, on the seat that *faced* the rear of the car, so that her captive-lover would be further tormented by the sight of her, compelled to accept his, his rival's, caresses.

Isaac Wolferstein was cruelly bound, fastened to the rear of the car, and made to stumble over the road, and often to be dragged, when the pace of the car carried him off his feet. Once or twice he almost fainted, for the soles of his feet were skinned—his captors had purposely divested him of his shoes and socks. The ants found out the bare, bleeding feed and added torment to his pain.

The city was astir as the car entered. The news was shouted from the car, that one of the accursed, who defied "The Lord, Apleon," had been captured, and was to be tortured in the Broadway.

*   *   *   *   *

The great open space was crowded with people. As, of old, the Roman populace gathered in holiday, theatre mood to see the Christians tortured and slain, so had this great concourse gathered about the beautiful Miriam, and her handsome lover Isaac Wolferstein.

One of the Kiosks, from which "Covenant" brands were worked, was opened, and the spring instrument was brought out. Apleon's chaplain was there, and in a voice heard clearly by everyone at the farthest remove from him, he asked:

"Isaac Wolferstein, will you worship "The Lord Apleon?"

Wolferstein was hoarse with pain and thirst, but lifting his head proudly, he looked the *"False Prophet"* full in the eyes, as he cried fearlessly:

"Never! Apleon, is a demon, and of his father Beelzebub!"

"Silence, you beast!" yelled his tormenter, and he struck him across the lips with the stick he carried. Then he turned towards the beautiful Jewess, saying:

"Miriam Cohen. Will you worship our Lord Apleon, and wear his brand?"

"Never!" she cried.

He spat at her, as he said, "Well, we shall see!"

He turned to Wolferstein again, saying: "Where has Cohen, the ex-priest, and that herd of disloyal pigs gone?"

"I will not tell you!" replied the captive, proudly.

"You defy me, so be it. Aha, aha!" The *"False Prophet"* laughed mockingly. Turning to some of the Apleon guards who were massed on two sides of the Broadway, he said:

"Strip him! and lash him——." He lifted his eyes to the sun, calculated how it would travel, then, with a fiendish smile, he indicated one of the pillars of the colonnade, "lash him there were the sun will reach him."

They tore the clothes from the fine form of the loyal young Jew. Then, when he was absolutely nude, they fastened him to the pillar.

A honey-seller stood in the crowd. An officer of the guards spied the man, and called him out. "Take a handful of that fellow's honey," he ordered one of his men, and lightly smear that foul Jew's back and shoulders, his face and ears too. Don't put it on thickly, but as light as you can, that the insects may find his flesh *through* the honey."

The officer's bidding was done. Then began as hideous a martyrdom for Isaac Wolferstein, as had ever come to a soul loyal to God. The flies, ants, and a score of other stinging things found him out. His honey-smeared flesh was black with them.

In his agony and torture he turned his eyes upon Miriam. "My darling!" he cried, as well as his dried leather tongue and throat would let him. "God will pardon you, surely, if you bend to circumstances, and wear the foul sign!"

"But I should never forgive myself, Isaac," she called. "And how could I meet Jehovah's searching eye, if I failed Him now. Courage, courage dear one!"

She knew, as we know, that Wolferstein meant no disloyalty to his God, but that he was momentarily beside himself with the agony of his torture and his love for her.

With a very suave, mocking smile, *"The False Prophet"* spoke across the six yards that separated him from Miriam, saying:

"Tell us where your father and that foul herd that went with him, are located."

"I will not, not even if you torture me to death," she cried.

"Wait until your torture begins, before you brag!" this to Miriam. Then turning to some of the soldiers, he cried: "Strip her, don't leave a rag upon her, and treat her from top to toe with that smearing of honey!"

Wolferstein shut his teeth sharply with the agony that swept over him at this order. In that moment he was unmindful of his own torture, in his dread contemplation of his loved one's shaming and torment. He shut his eyes that he might not see all that followed.

The brutal soldiery took a fiendish delight in fulfilling the order given them. They literally rent the clothes off the beautiful girl in strips and ribbons. Then when she stood absolutely nude before them, they smeared the beautiful form with the honey.

"Lash her to *that* pillar," cried Apleon's hellish deputy. He indicated a pillar, adding: "While they will both get the full benefit of the sun, they can see each other— lovers are never really happy out of sight of each other!"

There was a roar of laughter at this thrust.

We cannot—there is no need to detail all their sufferings. In less than two hours both were crazed with the blistering sun, and the ravening of the foul and biting insects.

Once, just before the crazing robbed him of coherent thought, the mind of Wolferstein travelled to the Psalm he knew so well from his childhood's days, and his black backed lips feebly murmured:

"Be not far from me, O God, for there is none to help me. Many bulls of Bashan have compassed me. I am poured out like water, my heart is like wax, it is melted within me. My strength is dried up like a potsherd; and my tongue cleaveth to my jaws; I am brought into the dust of death; for dogs have compassed me; the assembly of the wicked have enclosed me. Be not Thou far from me, O Lord: O my strength, haste Thou to help me. Deliver my soul from the sword; my darling from the power of the dog."

The lovers were alike, both past speech a moment later, and it looked as though they would soon be past consciousness. Not a single eye, apparently, in all that vast crowd, had cast a glance of pity upon them, no voice had been raised in sympathetic pleading for them. Devilism was the heart of all things, and it changed men and women into veritable demons. Their persecutors had been as fiends in their torturing, and the onlookers enjoyed the scene as of some fine sport.

And now it looked as though both were dying. Both were losing consciousness. The half-closed eyes were blood-shot; the lips were baked black, and hideously swollen; their mouths were open; and where the suffused blood—from the fierce knottings of the cords that bound them—showed blue and purple, the veins were swollen to the bursting point.

"The block and the axe!" commanded *"The False Prophet."* The grim things were brought.

"Loose the carrion!" came the next command.

A dozen hands were busy in a moment with the knotted cords. Miriam was the first to be fully released. Her eyes were closed; her breaths were heavy, slow throbs; her beautiful form bent and swayed; and the soldier who held her had to bear all her weight. He carried her to the block; then, waiting, glanced for instructions to where the officer of the guards, and *"The False Prophet"* stood.

An executioner, toying with his axe, stood by the side of the block.

"Off with it!" called *"The False Prophet,"* laughingly.

The soldier lifted the nude, insensible form of the beautiful girl so that her neck rested in the hollow of the block. He held her in position. The axe fell. The head rolled to the stone pave. A woman close by, caught the head by the hair, twisted her fingers well into the beautiful black swathes, and swinging the gory thing around her head, let it fly from her hand, shouting, as it hurled through the air.

"A kick-off, for the *first* team!"

The mob, among whom the head fell, began to play football with it. A moment later, the head of Isaac Wolferstein rolled to the pavement, and a second woman caught that and hurled it over the heads of the people in the opposite direction to that in which Miriam's head had gone.

"A kick-off," shouted the hurler of the head, "for the *second* team." *

*   *   *   *   *

This effort to trace Cohen and the fugitives had failed, but the knowledge soon came in, in four or five different ways. One of the wireless messages had brought a clue. Some traders brought in a fuller clue, and rapidly other news came to hand.

It soon became perfectly clear that there existed some kind of evident understanding between the various flee-ing crowds, and that their first place of united meeting was to be one of the agricultural colonies near to the old Kadesh-Barnea.

By this time the fugitives had had four good days start. Apleon ordered an enormous body of troops to go in pursuit, and to slay or capture the fugitives—

---

*May God arouse readers of this scene to reflect that there must be thousands living to-day, who will suffer thus hideously. Some, too, who to-day are members of churches, others, children of Christian Parents, many too, of the "Almost persuaded" among us.

capture, by preference, that they might be publicly tortured and beheaded.

Mad with the lust for blood, and that fouler lust of Religious revenge, the pursuing host sped southwards. The wondrous new motor-trains, that would career over hillocks easier than a thoroughbred hunter gallops over a turfy down, carried the expedition. There were a hundred trains of thirty cars each, besides a thousand or more single Motor-Cars, carrying from twelve to twenty persons. Worked on the then latest principle,— ether-driven—the cars and trains swept onward at the rate of a hundred miles an hour. Over head, travelling at the same rate, was a fleet of aerial war-ships, armed with infernal torpedoes, that if dropped into any town or community, would wipe out every living soul, and destroy the stoutest city, in a few minutes.

It looked as though the devoted band of Jews and Gentiles who had fled south were doomed.

Wild, exultant shouts of ironical laughter and unholy glee burst from the land and aerial pursuers, as they came within a moment or two (at their rate of travelling) of the fugitives.

The latter had seen them, heard them, and, as a body, were bowed in prayer for——. They scarcely knew what to ask, for deliverance or for fortitude, so that the essence of their prayer was *"undertake for us, Lord!"*

The sky lowered over their heads. They thought it was the aerial fleet hiding the sun—but the winged warriors were not *quite* come up over their place of gathering.

The prostrate refugees remained, to a man, upon their faces. Souls in direct dealing with God have no curiosity as to outside events.

Suddenly, like the hiss of ten thousand times ten thousand snakes, a rushing sibilation passed through the momentarily darkened air. At the same instant the earth trembled, and there was an awful, thunderous rumbling in the nether world.

Simultaneous with both of these phenomena there came yells and screams, then,—anon—silence.

The mass of refugees raised themselves, and stood silent with awe and thankfulness. Sheets of flame had rushed out of the heavens, overwhelmed the aerial fleet of vengeful pursuers, fired the vessels, and hurled men and machines downwards into a mighty gulf. For the trembling, and thundering of the earth had been the result and accompaniments of a terrible earth-quake, that now swallowed up the whole pursuing host—land and aerial, alike.

For a moment or two no sound came from the mighty crowd of miraculously-delivered refugees. Then, suddenly, one of the late priests of the Temple, a chorister-priest, burst into song:

"Sing unto the Lord, for He hath triumphed gloriously. The Lord is my strength and my song, and He is become my salvation: He is my God .... My father's God, and I will exalt Him. The Lord is a Man of war: the Lord is His name. Our enemy's chariots and his host hath He cast into the earth .... Thy right hand, O Lord, is become glorious in power: Thy right hand, O Lord, dashed in pieces the enemy. And in the greatness of Thine excellency Thou hast overthrown them that rose up against Thee; Thou sentest forth Thy wrath, which consumed them."

Almost in the instant of the starting of the song, thousands of Jews, (and Gentiles, as well) had recognized the Red Sea Triumph Song, and had joined the voice of the leader. What a swell of triumph it was! On, on they sang:

"The enemy said: I will pursue, I will overtake; my lust shall be satisfied upon them; I will draw my sword, and my hand shall destroy them. Thou didst blow with Thy wind, and they were destroyed.

"Who is like unto Thee, O Lord, among the Gods! Who is like Thee, glorious in Holiness, fearful in praises, doing wonders- Thou stretchedst out Thy right hand, the earth swallowed them. Thou in Thy mercy hast led forth the people which Thou hast redeemed: Thou hast guided them in Thy strength. The people shall hear, and be afraid: sorrow shall take hold on the inhabitants of Palestine. Fear and dread shall fall upon them: by the greatness of Thine arm they shall be as still as a stone; till Thy people, O Lord, till the people pass over, whom Thou hast purchased.

"Thou shalt bring them in, and plant them in the mountain of Thine inheritance, in the place, O Lord, which Thou hast made, in the Sanctuary, O Lord, which Thy hands have established. The Lord shall reign for ever and ever."

Three times over, led by the impromptu priest-precentor, that grateful, jubilant, delivered people sang the last sentence.

Then, as their song of praise finished, the leaders took counsel together as to what they should do next. It was the unanimous feeling, and expressed opinion, that Apleon would send forth other expeditions to destroy them, if he learned that they had escaped the fate of his aerial and land pursuit.

"I do not believe," cried Cohen, the chief spokesman

among the Jews, "that God Jehovah has permitted *one* of our pursuers to escape. God's judgments, like His mercies, are full and complete. Will Apleon, the Traitor to his covenant-word, ever know the fate of our pursuers? I believe not, unless anyone of us here retrace his steps to Jerusalem to tell him, and that would mean public torture and death to the tale-bearer."

He paused, and glanced around on the throng nearest to him, as he asked:

"Does anyone present know anything in the Scriptures relating to this present position, that will serve as a guide to our movements now?"

A tall, fine-looking man responded by lifting his right arm. He was asked to speak. He came forward and stood upon the hillock where Cohen stood. Holding aloft a Bible, he cried:

"Men and Brethren, of the stock of Israel, and Gentiles associated with them. I was a Christian minister, so-called, in Australia, when the 'Rapture' took place. I was *left behind,* because, though I could preach eloquently enough, and could keep my church filled to overflowing. I was not a converted man; I had been trained for the church, as my only brother had been trained for the bar. I never realized the need of conversion, my soul was filled with pride in my gifts, hence I was left behind when Christ came for His own,—and, among His own, thank God, were many 'Israelites indeed,' as well as Gentiles.

"Since my conversion, friends, (and though too late for the Rapture, yet still the glorious event took place within forty-eight hours of the Rapture) I have *studied* my Bible, to see what should happen. Everything *has* happened according as the New Testament has laid it down: The 'people of God,' the Jews, have built their Temple. They made their seven-year covenant with Apleon. The Anti-christ, the Scripture calls him.   At the end of the three and a half years (*half* of the covenant time) he orders the Sacrifice to cease in the Temple at Jerusalem—and everybody here knows how *literally* all this has happened.

"He has set up his own image to be worshipped, as was foretold, and God's ancient people, with those of us here who are Gentiles, have fled. We are here, to-day, here at this moment, living out exactly what the New Testament had all along prophesied would come to pass.   In that wonderful book, which deals with these times in which *we are now living,*—Revelation twelve, it says, that the faithful Jews, and others, *'were given two wings of a great eagle, that she might* fly into *the wilderness,* into *her place, where she is nourished for a time, and times, and half a time,* (three and a half years from now,) friends, which period will complete the seven years of Apleon's (Anti-christ's) reign.

"Now listen again to that same prophesy, friends: *'And the Serpent* (Apleon) *cast out of his mouth water as a flood, after* (the fugitives, us who are here today) *that he might cause them to be carried away of the flood. And the earth helped* (the fugitives) *and the earth opened her mouth, and swallowed up the flood which the dragon cast out of his mouth.'* Has not every item of this been actually fulfilled, has not God opened the earth and swallowed up the flood, and delivered us?   Then that wonderful prophecy goes on:

"*And* (the fugitives) *fled into the wilderness, where they had a place prepared of God, and where they should be fed for twelve hundred and sixty days,* (three and a half years.)

"I do not pose as a prophet, friends, but I cannot help thinking from all I read, some of which I have quoted to you, that God's mind for us is that we should make our way into the wilderness beyond here, where God's people of old time went, after God had swallowed up Pharoah's hosts, even as He has just swallowed up Apleon's hosts.   For, did you notice, in the word I quoted to you just now, it not only said *'the* wilderness,' but *'her place.'* It was the wilderness yonder there——"

He pointed Southwards with his finger.   "In Sinai; where Moses fled from the wrath of Pharoah; where Israel fled when pursued by the Egyptians; where Elijah fled from bloody Jezebel, and where, again and again, God's people have found shelter, so that God calls it *'her* place.' It comes to me, as I speak thus, that since Apleon's attempt to destroy us has failed, (whether he will learn that, or not, he will know that his punitive expedition does not return to him) his rage will be fixed against all, in every part of the world, who will not worship him, and his image.   So that the persecuted ones, in each land, against whom his rage shall blaze, will probably flee to some wilderness in their own land, while thousands of those who cannot flee will meet martyrdom.

"But wheresoever the wilderness shall be, whether down there in Sinai, or in that vast desert in my wonderful land of Australia, or in one or other of America's deserts, or the desert of whatever land it may be, God will, I believe, miraculously feed, as He miraculously fed the fugitive millions of Israel with manna, and fed Elijah with food from Heaven by ravens.   He could send 'manna' again, or any other food he pleased. Or he could as readily feed if he pleased, with one meal to last the three and a half years, as he could make his servants of old 'go in the strength of one meal for forty days.' "

There was a little more in this strain, then there followed a kind of general conference upon the matter in hand. The whole thing was too serious to be delayed, or trifled with, and, eventually, it was agreed to travel as swiftly as might be to the "Wilderness of Sinai," where waiting upon God, they would hope to be directed in any future movement, or be sustained by his wonder-working hand.

CHAPTER XVI

MARTYRED.

I T was three months since the image of Apleon had been set up in the "Holy" place in Jerusalem. Now all the world worshipped "The Beast," for the images had been multiplied until every town and city and almost every church, etc., had its own idol.

The world had begun by *"Wondering after"* the Beast, it gave itself up to error, despised the Truth, opened itself to receive the *"Strong delusion,"* the *Anti-*christ lie, so that the *worship* of the Beast himself, then of his image, became but just consequent steps one after the other.

In Ancient Roman days its Emperors took divine titles, accepted homage, worship, honor, all of which belonged, by right, to Deity alone. Augustus had temples reared for the worship of himself, and, through all the ages since, the remains of one of these temples (at Angora) has remained, and inscribed upon a great stone lintel is the significant word: "To THE GOD AUGUSTUS." Near by, in the same district, is a kindred inscription, "To MARCUS AURELIUS . . . . *by one most devoted to his Godhead."* Nero and Domitian, fiends of blood and lust, were styled, while they lived, "GOD," and "OUR GOD AND LORD."

And Apleon fulfilled, to the minutest letter, all that was prophesied of him as regarded his assumption of the divine. *"He will exalt himself,"* wrote Daniel *"and magnify himself above God. He will speak marvellous things against the God of gods. He will not regard any God, for he will magnify himself above all." "He opposeth and exalteth himself above all that is called God,"* Paul said, *"or that is worshipped; so that he, as God, sitteth in the temple of God, showing himself that he is God."*

Whatever may be the cause of it, the fact remains that ever since the Devil's lie in Eden was absorbed by, and ruined man, there has been a proneness, a latent tendency to idolatry in the human race. And the *manifestations* of this tendency have not been confined to peoples who in their recent past have been won from idol worship.

As late as the revolution days, in cultured, polished France, busts of Marat and others, were greeted in the streets with bursts of Hallelujahs, by the populace, and, even in the churches, all over France, the people sang odes and Hallelujahs, and bowed themselves before these busts, and at the mention of their names. Marat, especially was treated as divine and "was universally deified," and "divine" worship of his image was everywhere set up in churches.

And the "worship of the Beast" came about easily, and as the natural transition from the world's earlier adulation of the "Man of Sin."

Millions upon millions of his image, in the form of charms, were worn like the *eikons* of the Greek church. In the hour of death these *eikons* (likenesses) "of the Beast," were held before the eyes of the passing soul, as the crucifix was held, (in the old days before the destruction of the older ecclesiastical systems,) before the eyes of the dying Romanist and Ritualist.

In that first three months of the *second* half of the seven years of Anti-christ, much had changed in every

way in the world. Under the supreme dictation of
Apleon changes commanded by him were effected
throughout the whole world, in one week, that would
have occupied a century in the old days of the nineteenth
century, say.

Babylon the Great, which had long since been rebuilt,
had become the world's commercial centre.   It was
exclusively a *commercial* city, there was nothing ecclesiastical (Babylon *ecclesiastical,* the religious system had
been destroyed, when all *religious* head-ship had been
summed up in Apleon).

There was nothing military, in the New Babylon, and
though every vileness in the form of entertainment was
to be found in the great city, all this was but the recrea-
tive side of the life of the commercial people of the
world's metropolis.

Ever increasingly, during the 19th century, and the
first decade of the 20th, commerce had been growing as
clamorous and as exciting as the "horse-leech," never
satisfied, ever crying "give, give." It had clamoured for
a common currency, common weights and measures,
common code of terms, and a hundred and one kindred
things.

But it was in Babylon the Great, that the woman of
Zechariah v. 1—Commerce—had found all she had been
insisting for, through all the past years,—and it all
emanated from, and was centred in Apleon. And it was
all connected with worship. *"Covetousness, which is
idolatry."*

With the utter destruction of "Mystic Babylon," the
vast religious system, (whose destruction we have seen,)
there came a mighty impulse of commerce, and of consequent wealth to "Babylon the Great" the City

Apleon had made it his head-quarters. *"The kings of the earth lived wantonly with her."* Her wharves and warehouses—built on that wondrous Euphrates—were packed with *"merchandise of gold, silver, precious stones, of pearls, fine linen, purple, silk, scarlet, and all rare woods, and all manner of vessels of ivory, brass, iron, marble, cinnamon, odours, ointments, frankincense, wine, oil, fine flour, wheat, beasts, sheep, horses, chariots, slaves—and souls of men."*

Her vessels traded with the whole world. Her liners, travelling at 100 miles per hour, were in easy touch of every land. Her pride in her Maritime and commercial power, was overwhelming: "How much she hath glorified herself, and lived deliciously. . . . For she saith in her heart, I sit a queen!" Her aerial merchandise fleets, too, were amazing!

*   *   *   *   *

The three months had brought great changes to the trio in whom we are specially interested—Ralph Bastin, George Bullen, and Rose, his young wife.

Ralph, in quitting the editor's chair of the Courier, had received a handsome *doucier,* from Sir Archibald Carlyon, and this, at his special request, had been paid to him in the new paper currency of the time—there was a world-common currency, under the Apleon regime, as there was also a world-common code, weights and measures, etc.

He had also contrived to turn his savings into the paper currency. George Bullen had done the same, though in the case of each of them it had not been easy work. for both we.e marked men.

They knew themselves to be hated—and watched. Again and again they had narrowly escaped death, and each day they realized that it might be the last.

The news of the wondrous enthusiasm of the world's peoples gathered in Babylon and Jerusalem, in their new worship of the golden images of Apleon, had stirred London, New York, Berlin, Paris—*atheistical* Paris; and all other great world-centres, and in each city many images had been set up.

Though neither Ralph Bastin, or George Bullen had now anything to do with journalism—they could not obtain work of any kind because of the absence of the "mark of the Beast" upon their foreheads. But both were journalists by nature, hence when they knew that the image of the Beast was to be set up in St. Paul's on a given Sunday, they determined to be present to see how far this basest of idolatry had really laid hold of London.

The trio lived together in a little house, in a by-street in Bloomsbury. Rose would never allow her husband to go out without her; the times were too perilous, either for him to be in the streets, or for her to remain alone at home. In the actual language of Ruth, she had said to him:—

"Entreat me not to leave thee:—for whither thou goest I will go; where thou lodgest, I will lodge; . . . . where thou diest, I will die; . . . . the Lord do so to me, and more also, if aught but death part thee and me."

On reaching the Mansion House—the old building was still there, though used for another purpose—they were amazed at the excitement which prevailed in the streets. Thousands of excited people were moving westwards, many of them evidently bound for St. Paul's.

*Every*one seemed to be wearing the brand of the "Beast," and more than once our trio came very near to being set upon, for that they were defying public opinion, as well as the command of the All-Supreme Director of consciences as well as lives—Apleon—by the absence of the "Mark" upon them.

Arrived at the cathedral they had no difficulty in getting in, since the hour was early, and a rumour having obtained credence that the great idol was to be wheeled out upon the steps of the cathedral, the vast bulk of would-be worshippers remained outside of the huge building.

Presently those outside must have become acquainted with the falseness of the rumour for there was a tremendous rush into the building, until, in three minutes, it was packed to its utmost limits.

Ralph, George and Rose had secured seats, in the centre of the third row, almost under the great dome, for they wanted to get as perfect a view of the image as possible.

The hum of several thousand voices, as the gathered people gossipped about the image, made quite a volume of sound. Every eye was fixed on the great golden statue. It was a wondrous piece of work and the likeness of Apleon was an extraordinary one. The people who were seated far back could see only from the breast upwards. But those nearer (Ralph, and George, and Rose among them) who could see not only the whole figure, but the plinth and the pedestal upon which it stood, saw that the inscription on the plinth was the same as that which had been reported as upon the first image, the one set up in the Temple at Jerusalem—"I AM. THAT I AM!"

A shudder passed over our trio, as they read the blasphemy.

Now, suddenly, a richly-robed priest, holding a silver bugle to his lips, stood out on the altar steps. The shrill bugle call for "silence" rang through the great building, and a tomb-like hush fell upon the multitude.

Another priest, more gorgeously costumed than the first, came slowly forward chanting clearly and distinctly:

*"We believe in Man, in the Religion of Humanity, Man is God, and God is man. We believe that all the excellencies which of old, were attributed to the God of the Bible, were but sparks struck out of the goodnesses that were within the man Himself. Hence we no longer need to be Divine by proxy."

The organ rolled out a *gay* note to which the gathered thousands chanted a gay "Amen!"

"We believe," the priest went on in his chant— "that the living God, is the marriage of Force and matter, of Head and Hand. And we believe that the product of this co-ordination is in our Great Superman, the God of the Universe, Apleon, our Superior-God, and Him we worship and adore—"

The priest made a well-understood sign, and the whole mass of the people *knelt*—they were too crowded to prostrate themselves. The great organ pealed forth in some wondrous chordings, that were dying down into zephyr-like breaths, when the voice of the priest broke the comparative silence.

"This creed, in its essence, and often in its terminology is taken from a book already published, in which the religion of Humanism exalts man to the place of God. (Author.)

In harsh, commanding tones, he cried:

"You three rebels, kneel at once!"

The whole congregation lifted their eyes to see two men, and a beautiful woman between them, standing proudly, fearlessly, amid the great kneeling throng.

"Kneel, you apostate rebels!" thundered the priest.

For answer, Rose lifted her strong, powerful, beautiful voice, in a God-inspired spontaneous burst of *true* worship, singing:

> "All Hail the power of Jesus' Name,
> Let angels prostrate fall."

Ralph and her husband caught the inspiration and the musical key, and the trio had reached the "Bring forth the Royal Diadem," before the great congregation of blasphemers awoke to the full meaning of what the song of the trio meant. Then, with a roar like ten thousand lions, they shouted:

"Kill them! Murder them!"

The priest raised his hand, the bugler sounded "Silence." The old hush fell upon the people, instantly, and the priest, with a triumphant note ringing in his voice, and with an equally triumphant smile on his face, cried:

"We have anticipated the action of such rebels as these, and have prepared for them. Outside there has been already set up an automatically-locked scaffold—"

With a wave of his hand towards our trio, he cried; "To the block with them, unless they instantly worship."

Pointing with his long index finger to the three *Protesters,* he shouted: "Kneel!"

For answer they drew themselves upright, and with a ringing gladness began to sing:

"Crown Jesus Lord of all!"

Instantly they were seized, and hurried out of one of the side entrances. With the utmost difficulty a way was cleared for the passage of the priests and the three victims—the bugler going ahead sounding sharp notes of warning on his instrument.

They reached the front of the cathedral, at last. The whole of the space in the front, at the sides, and far away into "The Fan" was packed with a seething, excited mass of human life.

Twenty feet high, a light but strong scaffold had been rapidly, and practically silently, erected—the whole structure having all its separate parts fitted with automatic lockings. The scaffold stood just *out*side the railings that fenced the cathedral from the "Fan."

On the platform of the scaffold was a conical-shaped block, enamelled in a brilliant red. A huge fellow, leaning on the handle of a wide-bladed gleaming axe, stood by the side of the block.

The trio of *Protestants* were taken up the steps of the scaffold. Two priests accompanied them. The chief of the two priests, he who had led the chant in the cathedral, held up before the trio a silver figure of Apleon, about eighteen inches long, and, (amid the intense silence all around, his words were distinctly heard) cried: Will you worship God?"

"We *do* worship God—but we will not worship either the Anti-christ, Anti-God, or his image!"

It was Ralph who, in ringing fearless tones, replied, the other two responding with:

"Amen! Amen! to our God who sitteth on The Throne, and to the Lamb, for ever!"

A savage roar swept upwards from the maddened mass below.

Ralph was told to bow his head upon the block. He did so, while Rose sang clear and strong:

> "Am I a soldier of the cross,
> A follower of the Lamb,
> And shall I fear————"

The chief of the two priests, struck her heavily across the mouth and silenced her. At the same instant the executioner held aloft, by the hair, the severed head of Ralph Bastin.

Yells of delight, mingled with "Long live *our* God Apleon!" greeted the sight of the head.

George Bullen's head was now upon the block, while Rose, the light of a holy triumph in her eyes, unable to sing because of her bleeding mouth, shouted, "Jesus! Jesus! Precious Christ!"

She kept her eyes from the block, and turned slightly away, as the head of her dear one was held aloft amid the frantic delighted cries of the murderous mass below.

It was her turn now, and she turned rapturously towards the block. But before she could lay her head upon the blood-stained horror, the chief of the priests thrust her forward to the near edge of the floor of the scaffold, and, holding his hand up for silence, cried:

"Is she too beautiful for the block?"

He caught her up suddenly in his arms, and held her as high aloft as his strength would permit, as he shouted:

"Does any one want her, if you do, say so, and I will hurl her down!"

"Behead her!" roared a voice in the crowd, and thousands of voices joined in the cry.

The priest dragged her to the block and laid her neck in the hollow of it. There was a flash of steel in the sunlight, and the beautiful head rolled into the basket. The next moment it was being held aloft by the long, lovely hair, the people below yelling with joy.

At a sign from the priest, the bugler sounded for "silence." Then the priest cried:

"So shall die every rebel against our LORD GOD, *The Emperor!*"

With a wave of his hand towards the Cathedral behind him, he added:

"Our worship will be continued in our Temple and, for today, at least, worship will continue all day."

The fools, the dupes, flocked back to the cathedral— as many as could crowd in. Those who could not get in watched the bodies and heads of the three martyrs for God hurled down from the scaffold on the stones below.

Someone suggested the river, and six lengths of line were quickly got, and amid the howls of mingled execrations, and the notes of a fiendish joy, the three heads and three trunks were dragged down to the blackfriars end of the embankment.

Here men cut the clothes from the three bodies, and the naked forms were kicked into almost shapeless masses, before they were eventually hurled over the embankment into the swirling muddy Thames.

"He, (The False Prophet) had power . . . to cause that as many as would not worship the image of the Beast should be killed."

From this day there began a perfect reign of terror on the earth, for the vast bulk of the people who had yielded utter allegiance to the "Beast," and to his worship, became heretic-hunters. Natural affection appeared to be actually absent from the world, and sons and daughters betrayed fathers and mothers, husbands betrayed wives, wives husbands, and the friend his friends.

Thousands were beheaded every month, taking the earth over—men, women, and children, who had learned to trust God, and who waited for the coming Kingdom of Christ, when, having put down all enemies under his feet, he should begin his reign of a thousand years. These saved ones, and martyred ones, were "an innumerable multitude saved out of T H E great tribulation, from all nations, kindreds, and peoples, and tongues."

CHAPTER XVII.

A GATHERING UP.

A T this stage it seems well to the writer to gather together in a brief—but necessarily very fragmentary fashion—some of the chief events of the second half of Anti-christ's reign, and those immediately preceding the millenial reign of Christ. The object of this little volume, as well as its predecessor—"In the Twinkling of an Eye"—being chiefly to incite in the readers of the two books, a desire to look into the wonders of the 'After Events," we can only touch upon these things in the most disjointed fashion, many events, from necessity of space, being untouched altogether.

*　　*　　*　　*　　*

The two scenes recorded in previous chapters—the torture and beheading of Isaac Wolferstein and his beautiful *fiancee,* Miriam Cohen, and the beheading of three at St. Paul's—were duplicated many thousands of times, every town and city of the wide world had its own hideous tale of torturing and of death.

The effect upon the bulk of the people was to deepen "the strong delusion," as to Anti-christ, under which they laboured, so that they fed upon "The Lie," and became abject slaves in their wills and worship of the "Man of Sin."

The effect of the perecution and martyrdoms upon most of the believers—kingdom believers—was to

stiffen their faith, and to confirm their hope in the near
Coming of the Christ, to take vengeance upon his foes
and deliver his people.

The licentiousness and blasphemy of the times was as
a veritable atmosphere abroad, so that, affected by it, the
love of the many towards God waxed colder and colder,
until they flung off the last semblance of allegiance to
Him, in thought, word, or deed, and wholly given up to
"The Lie," they ripened rapidly for Judgment.

But amid the almost universal declension, there was
ever the remnant—Jew and Gentile—who "endured,
seeing the invisible," and strengthening their souls in the
special tribulation promise *"He that shall endure unto
the end, the same shall be saved!"*

And these endurers shall be God's witnesses unto all
nations. No suffering, privation, no spending or being
spent will be counted too much by these tribulation-time
witnesses; they will live only to serve God in witnessing.

The chief source of temptation and danger to the
"Kingdom Believers" will be from the ever multiplying
"False Christs." Each new imposter parading some new
notion, but each in turn, either publicly slain by order
of the "False Prophet," or mysteriously disappearing.
The only likeness of imposture in them all, existed in
their claim to be the Saviour who should deliver from
the awful days of tribulation which the would-be godly
were passing through.

A similar thing preceded the first advent of our Lord,
only *then,* the sole trust of these imposters was in their
own statements; but before the coming of Christ again
to the earth, when the cry will often be "Lo here is
Christ," and "Lo there is Christ," these imposters will

buttress their claims with the exhibition of supernatural powers.

The "remnant" of faithful Jews which we saw in our last chapter, escaping to the "wilderness," will be only a *remnant*. The main body of the Jews of the world will have concentrated themselves in Jerusalem, its neighbourhood, and parts of Palestine left to them after the partition of the land by Anti-christ. Dan. xi. 9.

It would seem as though the "remnant," meanwhile learn of God so intimately that they become the Evangelizers of the world, preaching the Gospel of the *coming kingdom of Christ*. Rev. xiv. 6, 7. Matt. xxiv. 14.

Among those Jews who were unable to escape with the "remnant," there are also others who are loyal to God, who would not worship the Beast or his image, many of whom are betrayed by their bigoted Jewish relatives. All these, alike, are delivered up to Antichrist and to his creatures, to be tortured and to be killed.

"Then shall be great Tribulation, such as was not since the beginning of the world to this time, no, nor ever shall be. And except those days should be shortened, there should no flesh be saved: but for the elect's sake, those days shall be shortened. Matt. xxiv. 21, 22. Dan. xii. 1. Jer. xxx. 7, 11, 14, 15. Zech. xiii 8, 9.

May it not well be that the imprecatory Psalms, otherwise so difficult to understand, in the virulence of their desires for vengeance, etc., are prophetic of these days of persecution and tribulation? As well, too, must be many of the *Prayers* of the Psalms, etc. Ps. xxv. 2. Ps. lxxiv. Ps. cxl. Ps. lxxix. Isaiah xxxv. 3, 4. Isaiah li. 12-15. Micah vii. 8, 9. Luke xviii. 7, 8.

The almost universal return of the Jew to his own

land, with all the aims of Zionism, and other kindred movements among the Hebrew people today is, curiously enough, not marked by the *religious* spirit, but purely *national*. The comparatively few pious souls (certainly not more than a quarter of a million, if that) who built the Temple, and afterwards flee into the "wilderness," or are beheaded rather than worship the Beast, or who, unable to get away in time, are beheaded for their loyalty to God, are now left out of future count in the history of the final fate of Jerusalem.

The city will probably be enormously enlarged and will come to embrace miles of suburbs, as London has absorbed towns as far distant, almost, as Croydon, in Surrey.

In the latter years of the great Tribulation there will appear to be a general rising of the nations against Jerusalem—against the Jews. It may well be, that all the powers will have become so indebted, *financially,* to the Jews, that there shall be an universal outbreak of Anti-Semitism, the real cause of the outbreak being inability on the part of the nations to pay their debts, when they shall make common cause against the Jew, hoping thus to clear off their debts, by the destruction of their creditors.

Preparatory to this great and final struggle, the great eastern boundary river, the Euphrates, will be dried up. The *literal* accomplishment of this great physical wonder, is an absolute necessity, if the vast hordes of the Eastern armies are to be marched to Jerusalem.

Even as those days of the end draw nearer and nearer God's people of that time will suffer more and yet more.

"Happy the dead who in the Lord do die from hence-forth. Yea (saith the Spirit) that they may rest from

their toils, for their works do follow with them. Ceased only that form of service which brings weariness, and have found perfect happiness in the ability to continue service without weariness."—ROTHERHAM.

While this is true of all the saints of all the ages, it is specifically true of those who, in The Great Tribulation, shall lay down their lives for God in faithful, enduring obedience.

And now the end draws ever more rapidly near. North, East, South and West of Palestine the armies of allies against Jerusalem close in upon her. Had the Jewish race been as loyally devoted to their God and His Word as they had been to Anti-christ the Deceiver, and his vile, promulgated laws, they would have, inevitably, recognized Psalms lxxxiii. 3, 4, as a prophecy of this time and the approach of their foes: "They have taken crafty counsel against thy people, and consulted against thy hidden ones. They have said, "Come, and let us cut them off from being a nation; that the name of Israel may be no more in remembrance.'"

But God has not forgotten His promises to Israel, and the time of her worst visitation, is to be His opportunity:

"Wait ye upon Me, saith the Lord, until the day that I rise up to the prey; for my determination is to gather the nations, that I may assemble the kingdoms, to pour upon them mine indignation, even all my fierce anger: for all the earth shall be devoured with the fire of my jealousy. Zeph. iii. 8. *"Now also many nations are gathered against thee (Zion,) but they know not the thoughts of the Lord, neither understand they His counsel: for He shall gather them as the sheaves into the floor."* Mich. iv. 11, 12. *"In that time, when I shall bring again the captivity of Judah and Jerusalem, I will also*

gather all nations, and will bring them down into the valley of Jehoshaphat, and will plead with them there for My people and for My heritage Israel, whom they have scattered among the nations, and parted My land. Joel iii. 1, 2, 9—12, 14. Zech. xiv. 1, 2. Zech. xii. 2, 3. Ps. lxviii. 1-3. Joel ii. 32.

Against the gathered multitudes of the armed nations—every devilish instrument of war then known, being brought to bear against the doomed city, doomed as the allies consider it—the Jews can bring but a comparatively feeble resistance. With seeming ease, Jerusalem would appear to be taken. *"The city shall be taken, and the houses rifled, and the women ravished; and half of the city shall go forth into captivity,* AND THE RESIDUE OF THE PEOPLE SHALL NOT BE CUT OFF FROM THE CITY." Zech. xiv. 2.

With great spoil, full of unholy rejoicing, their souls steeped in pride, their hands stained with blood, the victorious armies march to the great plain of Esdraelon to hold a mighty revel, and to prepare for any future event.

*   *   *   *   *

"How oft after anxious provisions of man
Flashes in with a silence God's unforseen plan!"

"God is a tower without a stair
And His perfection loves despair."

The residue of the people of Jerusalem, who were left in the city on the triumphant departure of the allies of Hell, were utterly broken in spirit. Their discomfited hearts will be being prepared for some word or sin. Will they then begin to see their national, as well as their

individual folly? Who can say for certain? But the
near-to-come events with them, would almost seem to
point to something like this. Certainly, God's unforseen
plan was about to flash in upon their despairing condition.

The world's peoples were *"fully ripe"* for the Judgment, and the *"sharp sickle"* of Judgment was now waiting to fall into the earth.

First come "signs," every sign a warning, yet the
peoples, the enemies of Christ, will not hear nor see.
*"Immediately after the Tribulation of those days shall
the sun be darkened, and the moon shall not give her
light, and the stars will fall from heaven, and the powers
of the heavens shall be shaken."* Matt. xxiv. 29. Isaiah
xiii. 9-10-13. Joel ii. 30, 31. Joel iii. 15. Rev. vi. 12-14.

"And then" (*after* the Tribulation, and *after* these
physical signs and disturbances) *"shall appear the sign
of the Son of Man in Heaven."* Matt. xxiv. 30.

What will this sign be? We cannot actually say. The
only Scriptural hint we know of is our Lord's own word
that "the Manifestation of His Presence will be as the
lightning which flashes from the one end of heaven to
the other."

It may be that this will occur while men are horrified
with the unnatural darkness, and that the "sign" will be
a sudden and momentary cleaving of the black heavens,
so that the glory of the Lord will break through, and He
will, for an instant, be revealed in close proximity to
earth. Will it be thus that the Jew will receive his sign
from heaven?

That which follows, and which should be rendered:
"Then shall all the tribes of the land mourn," points to
the connection of this verse with Zechariah's prophecy:

"And I will pour upon the house of David, and upon the inhabitants of Jerusalem, the spirit of grace and supplications: and they shall look upon ME *Whom they have pierced, and they shall mourn for Him, as one mourneth for his only son, and shall be in bitterness for Him, as one that is in bitterness for his firstborn."* Zech. xii. 10.

"And again, the manner in which Zechariah's prophecy is quoted in the Apocalypse may, perhaps, afford some slight argument in favour of the explanation of the sign suggested above, namely, that it is Christ Himself seen for a moment through a rift in the clouds, for John says, *'Behold He cometh with the clouds: and every eye shall see Him, and they also which pierced Him: and all the* TRIBES OF THE LAND *shall mourn because of Him.'*

"Thus the Jews, although they may not as yet understand all, will at least know that it was the Messenger of Jehovah whom they slew, and that in so doing they pierced Himself. And they will mourn with no feigned lamentation, but as one mourns for his first-born, nay, his only son. All their pride will have broken down; for the word will then have been fulfilled, *'I will take away out of the midst of thee them that rejoice in thy pride, and thou shalt no more be haughty because of My holy mountain. I will also leave in the midst of thee an afflicted and poor people, and they shall trust in the name of the Lord.'* Zeph. iii. 11, 12.

"Then will God look down upon the stiff-necked and rebellious people, whom long centuries of chastisement could not subdue, and lo! a remnant, broken-hearted and contrite, humbly confessing that *'all their righteousnesses are as filthy rags, that they are all fading as a leaf, and that their iniquities, like the wind, have carried them away.'* They long for the personal interposition of God their Father, and cry, *'Oh that Thou wouldst rend the heavens, that Thou wouldst come down!'* They are ready at last, for their Messiah. Christ has become precious to them: there is no need that He, the true Joseph, should longer refrain Himself. He had indeed said, 'Ye shall not see Me henceforth till ye shall say, *"Blessed is He that cometh in the name of the Lord."'*

"But that word withholds Him no longer; for now their eyes are waiting for the Lord their God, until that He have mercy upon them: their souls are watching for Him more than they that watch for the morning."

(PEMBER'S "GREAT PROPHECIES.")

Then shall He suddenly come, "His feet shall stand in that day upon the Mount of Olives, which is before Jerusalem on the east; and the Mount of Olives shall cleave in the midst thereof toward the east and toward the west, and there shall be a very great valley, and half of the mountain shall remove toward the north, and half of it toward the south. And ye shall flee to MY valley, when He shall touch the valley of the mountain to the place He separated." Zech. xiv. 4, 5.

In this great valley of His special making it is possible, probable, that our Lord will shelter His people, while He is destroying the hordes of Anti-christ. It is of this that Isaiah speaks: *"Come My people, enter thou into thy chambers, and shut thy doors about thee: hide thyself as it were for a little moment,* UNTIL THE INDIGNATION BE OVER PAST. *For behold the Lord cometh out of His place to punish the inhabitants of the earth for their iniquity."* And when that awful judgment shall be over—*"which shall burn as an oven,"* they shall come out of their shelter *"skipping as calves of the stall."* A wondrous figure of the frolicsome calves coming out of the darkness of their stalls into the glorious light, and into the full freshness of the luscious meadows.

All this time Anti-christ and his warrior hosts are camped in the plain of Esdraelon, preparing for a fresh attack that is to utterly demolish the Jews as a nation.

To Apleon, The Anti-christ, word comes of the appearance of Christ, and that He is espousing the cause of Israel.

Satan, and his colleagues, self-blinded, suppose that they can war with and overcome even Christ and His hosts of saints; and, determined to do this: *"the kings of the earth set themselves, and the rulers take* counsel together, against His Anointed." Psa. ii. 2.

Armageddon—the Valley of Megidda; "The Valley of Jehosaphat;" "Bozrah," all these names are mentioned as the scene of the great final conflict between Anti-christ and Christ, between the armies of the earth, and the translated Saints of God who return with Christ.

It is probable that the line of the encamped hosts of Anti-christ will extend from Bozrah, on the southeast, to Megidda, on the North-west. Is it we wonder, merely a coincidence that this should measure exactly 1,600 *Stadia,* the actual distance named in Rev. xiv. 16, as that over which the blood of the judgment wine-press flowed.

Surely Habakkuk's wonderful prophetic vision covered this great battle-field. "God came *from Teman,* and the Holy One *from Mount Paran."* The march of God's indignation would seem to be from Sinai, through Idumea, past Jerusalem, and on to the mighty field of Esdraelon's plain.

 Oh, what a scene it will be! The glory, the judgment! our Christ on His White Horse; His eyes a flame of fire; on his head many crowns (diamens,) vestured and girded with his title "KING OF KINGS AND LORD OF LORDS!" his bride is with Him—for the *"Marriage of the Lamb"* has taken place; the bride is every believer who has been gathered out of the world by the Spirit. You, who read this, he who writes this, if so be we are in Christ, *"looking for, and hasting the coming of our Lord,"* yes, we shall be there, we shall be His army.

"On white horses," whether literal horses or not does not matter, the term implies force, power, swift movement, even triumph. Christ's army will be a cavalry force. Like our Lord we shall wear no armour,—"clothed in fine linen, white, pure,"—we shall be immortal, *"no weapon that is formed against us shall prosper."*

Every enemy, every foe of Christ will be there. The earth-armies, the dwellers of the earth, Demon-possessed, will be blinded, deluded by the lie of the Anti-christ, and "The False Prophet." There is no madness or delusion into which the most rational of men will not run when they are demon-possessed.

"Outside the city, the battle takes place, for the city has become Holy by the recent presence of Christ. Not even a private soldier of Anti-christ's hosts is *inside* the city, for, it may well be, that Christ has already appropriated it.

"Outside the city, the wine-press is trodden!" wonderful figure! "Fully ripe," is said to be the condition of the *"grapes of the vine of the earth."* What grape, more so a *ripe* grape, can stand the weight of a man as his foot crushes down upon it? And the iron heel of "The Lion of Judah," crushes out the life of these gathered hell-led, hell-inspired hosts, *"and blood came forth*

*out of the wine-press of God's wrath, up to the bits of
the horses for distance of 1,600 stadia."* A river of
blood 160 miles in length, and reaching to the horses'
bits in depth! Even if it be taken as a figure only, the
figure is never so great as the fact it prefigures! *"The
land shall be drunk with blood, and its dust made fat
with fatness, for it is the day of Jehovah's vengeance,
the year of recompenses for the controversy against
Zion."* Isaiah xxxiv. 7, 8.

As a picture of the absolute triumph of God, on this
occasion, the Psalmist uses the most awful figure of any
in the Bible—THE LAUGHTER OF GOD! *"He that sitteth
in the Heavens* SHALL LAUGH: *the Lord shall have them
in derision."* Ps. ii. 4. *"God is not mocked!"*

"And the Beast (Anti-christ) was taken." The ring-
leader is first taken, not slain with the others. Taken
alive, he is cast into the Lake of Fire. The confidence
of the mighty host of Hell-inspired warrior hosts, had
been *"Who is like unto the Beast? Who can war with
him?"* But they see him taken, taken alive, taken without
being able to lift a finger against his captors. Tophet
had been prepared for him, and into that awful abyss he
sinks to rise no more.

*"And with him the False Prophet who wrought the
miracles in his presence."* Colleagues in evil on earth,
the two are hurled into the same Lake of Fire.

*"And the rest were slain with the Sword of the Sitter
on the horse,* (The Conquering Christ,) *which sword
proceeded out of His mouth." "He speaks and it is
done."*

"And a certain angel standing in the sun," has been
placed there ready to call forth the final actors on this
hideous battle-field, *"cried with a great voice, saying to*

all the fowls that fly in mid-heaven, 'Hither be gathered together to the great supper of God, that ye may eat the flesh of kings, and flesh of captains of thousands, and flesh of mighty men, and flesh of horses, and of those that sit on them, and flesh of all (classes of people,) both free and bond, and small and great . . . and the fowls were filled from their flesh." Rev. xix.

At the great and terrible conflict there are lightnings and thunders of unheard of force and might. *"The Lord of Hosts,"* says Isaiah xxix. 6, *"shall visit with thunder, with earthquake, and great noise, with storm and tempest, and the flame of devouring fire."* All through God's judgments, during the seven years of Anti-christ, aerial convulsions will be continual. One reason for this, during the later events will doubtless be to overwhelm and destroy the myriad *aerial* engines of war used by the senselessly deluded attacking hosts arrayed against Jerusalem and against Christ and His Saints.

"And there was a great earthquake, such as was not since men were upon the earth, so mighty an earthquake, and so great." Rev. xvi. 18. Jerusalem will be split into three parts, as a result of this earthquake. But the effect upon the nations is *utter* ruin,—*"the cities of the nations fell."* London, New York, Paris, Berlin, Chicago, every other city, collapses like a rent balloon, and the opened earth swallows up palaces and cots, men and women, and what the overwhelming and the falling shall not slay, shall perish in the awful conflagrations produced.

"And Babylon the great was remembered in the presence of God to give her the cup of wine of the fierceness of His anger." Babylon, the great, the colossal city of mighty splendor, re-built, as we saw earlier in this book,

will have become exclusively a *commercial* city. All the vice and sin and voluptuousness of all the vilest cities of the whole world, through all the ages, gathered up into one whole foulness, would be as virtue compared with the foulness and vice and voluptuousness of the Great Babylon.

"*Fallen, Fallen, Babylon the Great.*" May we gather from the twice-repeated word "Fallen," that the collapse comprises the two things "*Babylon, mystery!*"—the foul religious *system,* the false worship,—and also Babylon *the city?*

God does not settle His accounts every Saturday night as petty tradesmen do. Babylon had been garnering judgment for herself, from the beginning. And the cry of doom goes out against her, from Heaven.

"*Render to her even as she rewarded, and double the double according to her works; in the cup which she mixed, mix for her double; insomuch as she glorified herself and was wanton,* TO THAT PROPORTION *give to her torment and grief. Because she saith in her heart, I sit a queen and am not a widow, and shall see no mourning, therefore,* IN ONE DAY, *shall come her plagues, death, and mourning and famine, and with fire shall she be burnt, because strong is the Lord who hath judged her.*"

And never more after this shall the foul city arise.

Awful convulsions of the earth will take place all over the world. The whole configuration of the earth shall be changed. Mountains and islands, well known before, will disappear.

With all the other aerial and other convulsions of nature, a hailstorm, covering an enormous area, will be one of the horrors, when, putting the weight of the stones at the lowest average, they will probably be quite a hundred-weight each.

And so event will follow event in such rapid succession as to puzzle the writer how to place them wholly in consecutive order. Satan will be taken and bound for a thousand years. The *living* nations will have been judged as regards their treatment of the Jews, and as to their acceptance of the Gospel of the Kingdom.

On, on, on, event upon event, until the glorious millennial reign of Christ shall be ushered in.

But before anything of which we have written in these pages can come to pass, our precious, loving Lord must come into the air to take up His own people to Himself. For this every true Christian should be looking, waiting, watching,—and *working* while they wait, for He has said *"Occupy* till I come."

"So I am watching quietly
    Every day,
Whenever the sun shines brightly
    I rise and say,—
"Surely it is the shining of His face,"
And look unto the gates of His high place
    Beyond the sea,
For I know He is coming shortly
    To summon me.
And when a shadow falls across the window
    Of my room,
Where I am working my appointed task,
I lift my head to watch the door, and ask
    If He is come?
And the Angel answers sweetly
    In my home,——
"Only a few more shadows,
    And He will come."
"Even so, Lord Jesus! Come! Come quickly!"

"FINIS?" No! WAITING!"